# Salvage Yard Treasures of America

**Compiled by**
**Cars & Parts Magazine**

Published by
Amos Press Inc.
911 Vandemark Road
Sidney, Ohio 45365

Publishers of
**Cars & Parts Magazine**
The Voice of the Collector Car Hobby Since 1957

Cars & Parts Magazine is a division of Amos Press Inc.
911 Vandemark Road, Sidney, Ohio 45365

Library of Congress Cataloging-in-Publication Date
ISBN 1-880524-31-7

Other books published by Cars & Parts Magazine:

Automobiles of America

Corvette: American Legend, The Beginning
Corvette: American Legend, 1954-55 Production
Corvette: American Legend, 1956 Racing Success

Pictorial History of Chevrolet, 1929-1939
Pictorial History of Chevrolet, 1940-1954

How To Build A Dune Buggy

The Resurrection of Vicky

Peggy Sue — 1957 Chevrolet Restoration

Suzy Q. Restoring a '63 Corvette Sting Ray

Ultimate Collector Car Price Guide

Salvage Yard Treasures of America

Catalog of Chevy V-8 Casting Numbers 1955-1993

Catalog of American Car ID Numbers 1950-1959
Catalog of American Car ID Numbers 1960-1969
Catalog of American Car ID Numbers 1970-1979

Catalog of Chevy Truck ID Numbers 1946-1972
Catalog of Ford Truck ID Numbers 1946-1972

Catalog of Chevelle, Malibu & El Camino ID Numbers 1964-1987
Catalog of Corvette ID Numbers 1953-1993
Catalog of Mustang ID Numbers 19641/2-1993
Catalog of Pontiac GTO ID Numbers 1964-1974
Catalog of Thunderbird ID Numbers 1955-1993
Catalog of Camaro ID Numbers 1967-1993
Catalog of Firebird ID Numbers 1967-93
Catalog of Oldsmobile 442, W-Machines & Hurst/Olds 1964-91

# Contents

# Introduction

**W**ith the publishing of this book devoted strictly to salvage yards, we celebrate the uniquely All-American "junkyard." You won't find anything quite like the U.S. salvage yard anywhere else.

Thanks go out to the yard operators who took time from their schedules to guide us through their yards. Also, we send thanks to our "bird dogs," those *Cars & Parts* readers who pointed out obscure yards in their parts of the country, often taking time off from their jobs to join us during a visit or to serve as ambassadors of goodwill prior to our visits. We're grateful to all. Without their help, it would have been beyond the staff's ability to locate some of the yards featured here and to identify the many obscure makes and models pictured in this book. Also appreciated are the "tall tales" and anecdotes that made the vehicles all the more interesting to photograph and describe.

There are a few observations that we feel worth mentioning. With the world growing smaller and smaller, we found remnants of days gone by, i.e. enclaves where the spirit of American enterprise is rich and thriving – men and women defying odds to make a living selling vintage tin despite civic and governmental restrictions that make their way of life uncomfortable at times and seemingly impossible to continue in the future. We believe salvage folk are classic recyclers

as they find worth in the discarded. And, they provide a very valuable service to car restorers. Certainly, their demise would be disheartening and a definite threat to our continued enjoyment of old cars.

On a lighter note, with the publishing of this book, we are nominating Leon Thompson, Leon's Auto Parts, Leon Va. as the unofficial spokesperson of all independent salvage operators. Leon seems to have a saying for everything. He's like a radio, but you can't turn him off. We'll leave out some of his more prophetic sayings so you can catch a few firsthand when you pay him a visit. A classic Leon is his take on chronic complainers who visit his yard and see every aspect of securing old car parts as a problem. "They complain about the weather, the amount of walking, what a pain it is to remove parts and, ultimately, the asking price," Leon says "Whinny butts aren't welcomed here. Here in Virginia, men are men and the women are damn glad of it." Need we say more?

In addition, we must pass on Leon's five "ought" words which he feels describe the successful restorer. "A restorer *thought* it, *sought* it, *bought* it – then *brought* it home where he *fought* it." Right on Leon.

Everywhere we went to visit and photograph caches of old cars and parts, we were told of visits by people who had traveled great distances to search a particular salvage yard firsthand. Old car

Gene Snyder, one of the proprietors of Snyder Bros. Garage & Auto Wrecking, Whitney, Texas (featured on page 79), sent us this priceless photo of his "father Albert leaning on a 1938 Nash." Albert Snyder "was born in Springfield, Ohio on July 29, 1919 in a covered wagon. He was 12 years old when he traded his pocket watch for his first Model T. Later he traded it for a Nash." Gene says his "Dad loved old cars and could tell you most anything you needed to know about them. So, as you can see, we [brothers] have had a little motor oil in our blood for a long time." It's a compelling photo and we just had to use it.

types are a mobile bunch with many spending their vacations chasing rare parts and it seems that each and every yard has had, at least, a few car collectors from "out in California," Wisconsin and overseas, etc. In retrospect, we may not fully appreciate the value of the resources these independent operators provide nor do we understand how desirable our American cars are in the international marketplace. Almost every yard featured here has had Germans, Swiss and other European visitors.

In our travels, we discovered a non-traditional method of selling vintage cars and parts that was unheard of 10 years ago. Several yard owners have geared up to sell cars and related parts on the Internet while others are designing web pages for posting in the near future. The electronic sales scheme has not been fully time-tested and we wait to see the results. The positive aspects would be the opportunity for hobbyists to identify rare and valuable parts sources right at their finger tips. The downside, many say, is finding an acceptable replacement for the traditional visual inspection that they have learned to trust over the years.

That reminds us of another interesting method of selling old cars and parts. We didn't attempt to count the salvage yard operators who vend cars and parts at swap meets. But it appears there is an increase in the number who are hitting the swap meets to sell, while others sim-ply use the meets as a way to keep abreast of current buying trends. Those we have spoken with are usually car people themselves, just like you and me, who enjoy old cars to the max.

As you thumb through this book, you'll find stories about old car caches located across broad sections of the country, but certainly not all. Hopefully, we will be able to visit others in the near future and come out with another edition. With each story, there's a detailed instruction block to make your travels to these yards easier.

Surveys that we have taken of *Cars & Parts* readers indicate salvage yard stories are among their favorites. Many readers plan their vacations and travel schedules using these stories as a guide. Or they use a salvage yard directory that we publish from time to time. You'll find the most up-to-date listing available in the back of this book. This list is the most complete listing you'll find anywhere of salvage yards that cater exclusively, or at least to an appreciable degree, to the old car restorer. If you know of a yard that you feel is worthy of inclusion in this list, please contact us by phone toll-free at 1-800-448-3611 or by writing to Cars & Parts Magazine, 911 Vandemark Rd., P.O. Box 482, Sidney, Ohio 45365.

Now, have at it. We hope you enjoy this book as much as we enjoyed producing it.                    – Ken New

Photos by the author

1. Becky and George A. Philbates, Jr., New Kent, Va., operate the largest vintage car salvage yard on the east coast. George opened the yard for business in 1955. He stocks salvageable cars that are 15 years old and older.

## "I may not be the cheapest, but I probably have it," says this east coast salvage yard owner

# Philbates Auto Wrecking

## New Kent, Virginia

2. Although this 1959 Dodge sitting in front of Philbates' garage represents the epitome of garishness, there's a frank and unassuming quality about it that makes it very desirable. We didn't expect to find a baby swing, at right, for sale at a salvage yard, but there it was – probably one from a collector series.

by Ken New

If you ask George A. Philbates, Jr., the owner of Philbates Auto Wrecking, if he has a particular car or part, he rarely hesitates. Philbates, the man with a photographic memory, will answer in a flash. And, since he knows his inventory by heart, he never wastes time sending one of his four yard men off in the wrong direction. With a few words, and more importantly a walkie-talkie in hand, Philbates directs his men into his cache of nearly 8,000 cars to retrieve a part or check on the condition of a car. Occasionally, the second walkie-talkie will crackle as more specific directions are needed – and the "computer center" never hesitates to supply more detail. In fact, it seems like Philbates is intimate with every blade of grass and rusty hulk on the 37-acre tract of land.

From his office, Philbates directs 50 or so forays daily. "Sometimes, it's a hubcap. Sometimes they want the whole thing," says the New Kent, Va. yard operator, who traces his lineage back 200-plus years to the early settlers of the region – the historically significant Chesapeake Bay area which includes the military academy at West Point and the

3

4

3. The well worn path, a little muddy the day we visited, leads past stacks of hubcaps. The deeper you go, the older the caps.

4. An accommodating Philbates walked through a misty rain to relate how he acquired each car in the yard. Philbates has a photographic memory and remembers exactly how he acquired every unit in his collection. A crew of four yardmen armed with walkie-talkies keeps in contact with Philbates as he directs them among 8,000 cars to salvage rare and valuable parts. A stub-nose '52 Ford heavy duty truck provided a leaning post as Philbates posed for this photo.

## ABOUT THE YARD

Philbates Auto Wrecking, Inc., P.O. Box 28 – Hwy. 249, New Kent, Va. 23124, phone 804-843-9787 or 804-843-2884 is owned and operated by George A. and Becky Philbates. Philbates is located directly East of Richmond, Va. If you are driving from the west, take I-64 toward Richmond (take the I-295 loop around Richmond and get back onto I-64) then get off the freeway at Exit 220 (West Point). Drive three miles to the traffic light. Turn left onto Hwy. 249. Philbates is a short distance ahead on the right. Hours are 9 a.m. to 5 p.m. weekdays and 9 a.m. to 2 p.m. Saturdays. Bring your own tools to pull off your own parts or Philbates will do it for you. The Chesapeake area is very scenic and Philbates is a great place to scrounge for parts while on vacation.

colonial Williamsburg community where early American lifestyles and industries are practiced.

The lineage of Philbates Auto Wrecking began in 1955 when Philbates, a typesetter for a newspaper in Charles City Co., began selling car parts for additional income. Initially concentrating on selling parts from newer model cars, Philbates soon realized that his stock had to be different to draw customers from as far away as Richmond and Newport News. Once Philbates had defined himself as a supplier of vintage automotive parts, customers began traveling great distances to shop at his yard, including old car owners from European and Asian countries who stop in to visit and stock up on critical mechanical as well as cos-

metic parts for their American-built cars. They say it's tough to find parts for U.S. cars overseas. Others have come only to photograph cars that they have never seen before.

In 1964, Philbates moved up the road to the current location where his inventory of vehicles ranges from a 1924 IH truck up to vehicles of all types that duck under a 15-year cut off point maintained by Philbates. "There's a few '30s and '40s cars, more '50s, and a lot of '60s and '70s cars," says Philbates who punctuated his comment with "I may not be the cheapest, but I probably have it."

Philbates and his wife of 13 years, Becky, have been approached by land speculators who want to purchase the land, crush the cars and develop the

acreage for homes, etc. So far, the Philbates have resisted the urge to sell, citing the welfare of their loyal employees. One has been with Philbates for 25 years. "When the yard was started in 1955," Philbates says, "there wasn't a house along this stretch of road." Now there are houses springing up everywhere, and Philbates, now 65 years old, speculates that eventually when he's out of the picture, his four children will cave in and sell. None have any interest in continuing the business.

Customers are allowed to pull parts at Philbates once they have checked in with the "computer center." Bring your own tools and expect to spend an hour or so listening to the amusing stories that this very friendly and accommodating couple have to tell. ∎

5. A 1939 Ford Standard two-door sedan rests comfortably a short distance from Philbates' garage. Philbates' prices for complete cars are competitive.

6. Hiding under a shed and a bunch of debris, this 1950 Plymouth Special Deluxe Station Wagon at Philbates represents the least purchased Plymouth model in 1950. Only 2,057 units were built. It was the last wood-crafted body offered by Plymouth. The body maker was the U.S. Body & Forging Co., Franklin, Ind. Philbates wants $2,500 for the project.

7. A late '40 Nash with four doors has most of its parts intact. Only a few cosmetic items have gone to new homes.

8. A 1958 Edsel serves as a "catch-all" for miscellaneous parts and other stuff of questionable value.

9. Philbates says he drove this 1955 Chrysler Crown Imperial into the yard some 15 years ago.

10. Ford's first two-door hardtop was in 1951. This Victoria is out of clear sight due to the dark canopy of trees that flourishes at Philbates.

11. Another inhabitant of the deep at Philbates is this 1950 Chevy pretend woodie. The built to look like a wood-constructed body is actually only steel shaped and painted to look like wood.

12. A Henry J from the early '50s wears the marks of designer Howard "Dutch" Darrin but not its grille and hood. The lightweight floundered in an American market that wanted bigger cars, and thus it was a lightweight in sales. The light bodies were popular with drag racers in the '60s.

13. Only in recent years have the 1958 Chevrolet Impala models garnered the respect they rightfully deserved. Most units like this two-door hardtop suffered from neglect and ended up in salvage yards.

14. 1960 Lincoln four-door hardtop needs only a few repairs to get it on its way.

15. It looks like roots from the old beech tree have raised this '55 Packard from the mulch of leaves. Lots of rare parts are left for gleaning.

16. No obvious subtleties that differentiate a 1946 from a '47 or from a '48 can be seen on this baby blue coupe from Chevrolet. However, the body is not too bad.

17. This venerable Ford wrecker winched and whined carcasses into Philbates yard in the '50s.

18. A 1960 Chevy plain-Jane four-door is almost hidden in the underbrush and fallen leaves in Philbates' New Kent, Va. salvage yard. It has a decent body and sheet metal to offer. Most complete cars at Philbates are priced at $300.

19. Once proud and speedy little '50 Olds coupe suffers from gross neglect and would have been crushed at most salvage yards, but not at Philbates' where long lives in retirement are guaranteed.

20. Although Philbates has cars that range into the '80s, this 1970 Mustang coupe was one of the newest we saw. The engine was gone but most of the car was still hanging around.

21. A DeSoto four-door from the late '40s is a bit down and out, but there are still parts aplenty for restorers to scrounge from this rare and unusual model.

22. In the midst of this photo, you'll find the remains of the oldest vehicle at Philbates, a 1924 International truck that has been converted into a stationary powerplant.

23. One of the more interesting bodies at the Philbates yard is this 1951 Ford station wagon. It is complete except for the wood and can be bought for a fair price.

24. Near the end of our visit, as we were leaving, we turned and shot this photo of a bunch of newer vehicles and a few oldies.

Photos by the author

1. Leon Thompson, Jr., an animal lover and salvage yard operator, stands in front of the old family dwelling where his father Leon, Sr., a carpenter, sheltered his wife and four kids and discovered that he could make a better living by supplying car parts. The salvage yard business began in 1962. The dog's name is Barney.

## One of the biggest yards in the country – and possibly the best mapped

by Ken New

# Leon's Auto Parts

## Leon, Virginia

Who would have imagined that within an easy two hour drive of our nation's Capitol that there would be a salvage yard with so many vintage cars you'd be lucky if you could inspect every one in a day's time? But, there is such a yard and, indeed, it takes all day to do justice to the cache of cars at Leon's Auto Parts, Leon, Va.

Leon's is run by Leon Thompson, Jr., an amiable 43-year-old who has a penchant for old wheels and "banjo pickin." Thompson says there are 10,000 cars and trucks scattered out along the wooded hillsides behind his garage. Most are '50s and '60s American-built cars. A few date back to the '20s. Others range into the '80s.

Interestingly, if you were casually motoring along US 29, a scenic stretch of highway that winds north into Washington, D.C., you could easily miss the collection of cars entirely – especially when the summer foliage is full. Leon's has been in operation since the early '60s and Thompson loves to tell the story of how his father started the business.

"It all started," he begins, when Leon Thompson, Sr., a carpenter in between jobs, was forced to find shelter for his wife and four children one night in 1961 when his car broke down as they were passing through Leon, Va. Fortunately, lodging for the night was found nearby at a farmhouse – that "just happened" to be

2. Caretakers to some 10,000 cars and trucks, Leon Thompson, Jr. (right), and Charles Johnson, Leon's one and only employee, enjoy an existence envied by many old car followers. The truck is Leon's project in progress. It's a '47 Ford with a ton of modifications. Thompson says he has 50 hours of work in the hood hinges alone. He modified his first car when he was 14.

for sale. The next morning, Leon, Sr. got his ailing car running and the family went on its way. A week later, he returned and bought the farm hoping his carpentry skills would continue to put food on the table. Things were looking better for the Thompson family. They had a roof over their head, but car ailments persisted and a few more bouts with the old plug ensued before he realized the people around Leon, Va. needed a place where good used auto parts could be purchased. So, in 1962, he dragged home an old car, parted it out and made more money selling its parts than he could make at carpentry. Soon, the yard was on its way to being one of the biggest in the country and Leon, Sr. quit pounding nails.

Leon Thompson, Jr. took over the business in 1983 and set about getting the yard organized – a task his father never undertook. The inventory and mapping of the cars, which took two years of Thompson's spare time, has been a real time-saver to car collectors who frequent Leon's. When they enter the yard, Leon presents them with a copy of his map, then directs them out the back door where the cars are stored and the "Wall of China" begins. The "Wall" is a row of 200 school buses that are stacked nose to tail circling the entire yard. The buses serve two purposes, Thompson says. One, they offer storage for excess parts and, two, they effectively regulate unauthorized movement in and out of the 100-plus acre facility.

Shoppers at Leon's are allowed to pull their own parts. Bring your own tools. You might want to pack a lunch as well. There's a lot to see and a lot of valuable parts for the taking. Keep your map handy and don't loose track of where you are. Better yet, don't plan to hang around after 4 p.m. You could spend an unpleasant evening treed by the yelping dogs that Leon turns loose in the yard at night. ∎

## ABOUT THE YARD

**Leon's Auto Parts, Hwy. 29, Leon, VA 22725, phone 540-547-2366 is owned and operated by Leon Thompson, Jr. Known as "The Walking Man's Friend," Leon's is located southeast of Culpeper, Va. on Rt. 29. To pinpoint Leon, VA on the map, look in the middle of the quadrangle formed by I-66, I-81, I-95 and I-64. Leon's Auto Parts is roughly 75 miles southwest of Washington, D.C. and 30 miles north of Charlottesville, Va. Business hours are 8 a.m. to 4 p.m. Monday through Friday and from 8 a.m. to 12 p.m. on Saturday. Gates are closed from Noon to 1 p.m. for lunch.**

3. Just inside the door to Leon's Auto Parts hangs an aerial view photo of the yard. It was shot several years ago when the trees were much smaller. A similar shot would be impossible today. Leon feeds eight animals; seven dogs and one cat. This cat's name is "O." Yes, just "O" – but that's another story.

4. Leon Thompson, Jr. stands ready to explain the large map hanging behind him. Pasted on flat windshields is a gigantic map that marks the location and make of every car in the yard. Thompson holds a smaller 8-1/2 x 11 copy like the ones he gives to his customers when they enter the yard. The location of every car in the yard can be determined quickly. The map is a little intimidating at first, but it works very well once you get used to it. It took Thompson almost two years of spare time to compile the details of this project – a task his father, Leon Thompson, Sr. never found time to do before he turned over the yard to Leon, Jr. in 1983.

5

5. A fence row of cars along the south edge marks the boundary of Leon's collection of cars and trucks that ranges from the '20s to the '80s.

6. Leon's has a bunch of hubcaps hanging from the ceiling. These are not culls that are dented and unrestorable.

7. The exterior appearance of the post-war DeSoto models ran without changes from 1946 through the '48. This coupe appears to have never been repainted or dented before finding its way to Leon's, yet it sufffers from slight surface corrosion.

8. A couple of Willy Jeeps sits in an adjacent lot to Leon's main storage lot.

6

7

8

9. The hints of real wood construction in station wagons were almost gone at Chevrolet by 1954, save for the ribbed tailgate which was actually made of steel.

10. In retrospect, it's a bit strange that the '56 Mercury, a real looker with a good reputation in its day, has never really caught on with the collector crowd like some of its cousins.

11. Brock Strickler was spending his day off from work shopping at Leon's for parts for a '51 Chevy his dad had given him. Strickler took some stainless trim from this '52.

12. From the different colors that split at the cowl, it appears this '55 DeSoto's front sheet metal had been replaced prior to its arrival at Leon's.

13. An old three-quarter ton Stude put out to pasture retains its handsome demeanor in retirement.

14. Here's an example of the last of the outrageous finned Buicks – a 1959 two-door hardtop. By '60 the fins were clipped and less pronounced; by '61 they were history.

15. This '51 Mercury four-door has sat on the ground long enough for the saplings to hem it in. This car shows up as item no. 4703 on Leon's map.

**16.** A couple of Packards from the '40s still have a number of usable parts to yield to a restoration in progress.

**17.** Built when crew cabs were really seriously functional, this GMC piece of fire equipment from the '40s is absolutely charming. Wouldn't you love to tool this monster through the Washington D.C. traffic 75 miles north of Leon's yard?

**18.** Stripped of most of its identifying trim, etc., this '58 Chevy Impala could still give up some sheet metal for use as patch panels.

**19.** In similar condition, this '57 Chrysler has quad headlamps. Not all '57 Chrysler models had quads that year.

20. A Studebaker Hawk Gran Turismo from the early '60s is down and out at Leon's.

21. It's surprising that a fan of the '39 Dodge from the Deluxe series hasn't bought the optional bumper guards for his pride and joy. They are factory original. All that remains of the optional fender-mounted parking lights are the bases.

22. Little of the distinguishing details that one needs to put an ID on this late '40 Ford coupe remain.

23. Which Dodge does this hood fit – a '55 or '56? Note the two pieces of chrome in the middle – that's a '56 feature. Also, there are no holes for the large V that designated a V-8 engine, so it must be a '56 six-cylinder hood.

24

25

24. The paint is fading on this boxy '53 Olds but it still has a number of usable parts aboard.

26. Unfinished 1956 Chevy project waits for someone to complete the job or to salvage her out completely. The body is fairly sound.

Photos by the author

1. The Clinkscales crew poses in front of the customer entrance to the salvage yard. David Banister, vintage cars and parts manager, is at left. Next is Terry and Ron Meeks, joint business managers and Sonny Clinkscales, owner. The '55 Ford F-100 is owned by part-time employee, Richard Luper, not shown.

# Clinkscales Garage & Recycling

## Belton, South Carolina

## Sandy South Carolina soil provides good footing for storing old cars and trucks

by Ken New

Clinkscales Garage & Recycling is a recycling center where a couple of hundred cars are crushed and scrapped weekly. Fortunately for collectors and restorers of vintage cars, David Banister, the man in charge of purchasing, has a passion for vintage tin. In the process of acquiring cars for Clinkscales, Banister has the advantage of examining every vehicle that enters the yard. "By splitting out the old stuff" from the run of the mill scrappage, Banister says, those cars that are of interest to the collector market are identified and saved from the crusher. This interesting buying in bulk, then separating the chaff from the wheat method, has allowed Clinkscales to accumulate "between 550 and 600 older cars" to sell as complete cars or as parts. Most are from the '50s and '60s, although some date back into the 1930s. Others range up into the '70s.

Like a lot of salvage operations, Clinkscales came from humble begin-

2. It's a 300, but it's not a letter car, although still somewhat rare. The '64 Chrysler from the 300 series is often confused with the high-powered upscale luxury 300s. It found only 13,401 buyers in '64.

3. Solid bodied 1953 Ford sedan delivery appears to be an abandoned project. The front suspension has been clipped and readied for an independent suspension upgrade.

4. Saddled up in style and comfort, a 1958 Ford Ranchero at Clinkscales has vinyl top, power steering and brakes and air, plus a solid body.

5. This mostly original 54,000 original 1950 Chevy slope back stayed in the same family until 1996 and passed South Carolina road inspection in 1995. It has received a repaint and the upholstery has been gone through.

6. A sleeper in the works. Sonny Clinkscales is building this 1948 Austin Princess as his personal road machine. Current work to date includes fitting an AMC Pacer front suspension and a Ford 302 mill teamed to an FX transmission.

## ABOUT THE YARD

Clinkscales Garage & Recycling, 2433 Hwy. 252, Belton, S.C. 29627, phone 864-338-6944, is owned by Sonny Clinkscales. The president and operations managers are Ron and Terri Meeks. David Banister is the vintage cars and parts manager. Clinkscales is located 12 miles east of Anderson, S.C. at the intersection of Hwys. 252 and 20 near Craytonville. From I-85 travel south on Hwy. 76 to Anderson. Veer right onto Hwy. 252 and proceed to Clinkscales, which is approximately four miles out of town. Weekday hours are 8 a.m. to 5:30 p.m. (EST). Saturday appointments must be made in advance.

nings. Owner Sonny Clinkscales says he "started the business in 1957, then went broke." A year passed and he was back in business again operating out of a 20 by 30 barn on the old homestead just up the road from the current address. As time passed and the business prospered, he added on to the barn, then moved to the current location in 1974. Nearing retirement a couple of years ago, he turned the business over to his daughter Terri and son-in-law Ron Meeks. Terri jokingly refers to herself as a "junkyard princess," alluding to her early childhood spent in and around the yard.

Clinkscales hasn't always solicited business from the old car market on a national basis. Up until 1986 when Banister came on board, after a stint in the U.S. Air Force as a military policeman, Sonny Clinkscales had operated the business primarily as a used parts and recycling center, even though he has always loved old cars and collected them.

And if the photos aren't enough to lure you to investigate this South Carolina yard, there are other attractions that make this a fine place to shop for old cars and parts. The climate is generally bearable, even in winter. The soil is sandy, so run off of ground water is good. No puddles to slosh through or to help generate extensive rust in the cars. Then there's the Southern hospitality. The Clinkscales are among the friendliest you will find anywhere. Practically every member of the staff took time from his or her schedule to tour the yard and point out interesting stock on hand. ∎

7. The extra nice condition of this '65 Ford F-100 custom cab makes one wonder why it was parted out. Old cars and parts manager David Banister and Sonny Clinkscales were in the process of upgrading an older truck using this '65 Ford F-100 custom cab as inspiration, but final plans called for a crew cab and the beautiful cab was left sitting high and dry.

8. No matter how you dice it, the '68 Mercury Cyclone GT has the lines of a winner. From the factory, the 390 with four-barrel pumped out 325 horses. It has bucket seats.

9. It seems that old Cadillacs are getting more popular as time passes. This is one of Cadillac's initial postwar offerings, a '46 coupe.

10. A trio of Fords waits adoption. At left is a '51 four-door sedan. Next door is a '52 and a restorable '55 F-100 with front sheet metal missing.

11. David Banister retired from military duty and came to Clinkscales with a mission in mind – recycle old cars. Here he assesses the condition of a '58 Cadillac two-door hardtop. Quad headlamps appeared first throughout the Caddy line in '58.

12. A '55-56 Mercury hood has been pressed into duty to keep the Rocket 88 engine dry in this '55 Olds. Any car stored in the big yard, the main storage lot, can be parted out.

13. Wearing U.S. Army stickers, this old tank, a 1964 Buick Wildcat convertible, needs little to be combat ready. A healthy percentage of the cars at Clinkscales can be made roadworthy in short order.

14

15

16

17

18

14. The four-door hardtop was offered in the Impala and Bel Air lines only in 1960. The single strip of trim above the rear wheel opening identifies this one as a Bel Air. The Impala featured two strips with complementing paint color in between.

15. Only the tailgate showed major damage on this restorable red '69 Ford Ranchero. Hood scoop was a Ranchero GT item, but this scoop is a bit too shallow to be correct and probably left the factory on a late-'70s Mustang.

16. Clinkscales is paying last respects to this once stately '40 Packard hearse by keeping it away from the crusher. It would take a lot to resuscitate this one.

17. This 1956 Lincoln Capri two-door hardtop is ready to donate its vital parts to a fellow Lincolnite in need.

18. This '46 Ford is GI issue. Note the headlight guards and the fading numbers on the bumper. Other military features are the overdrive trans. and instrument panel with flip switches instead of pull switches. Fort Jackson is some 100 miles away in Columbia.

19. Fairly complete except for wheel covers and abused window glass, this 1948 Cadillac from either the Series 61 or 63 groups utilizes the "B" body.

20. 1949 Pontiac Streamliner four-door sedan sat neglected for several years before being brought to Clinkscales.

21. An almost comical look with its tongue sticking out of its mouth was the result of Studebaker updating its '55 line. This Commander wagon is a late issue, as Ultra-Vista wraparound windshield which was introduced on sedan and sedan-based cars built after Jan. 1, 1955. Fortunately for the sake of the sleek lines, the coupe and hardtop models escaped the new bug splatter.

22. Always a favorite of the author, the '50 Olds 88 shared sheet metal with several other marques in the GM lines. Save for a crusty exterior, this four-door sedan is not a bad looker.

23. Save for its hood, punched out possibly for brightwork cabbaged from a late '60s Chevelle or Camaro SS hood, and a little surface rust, this 1956 Chevy two-door post has fairly straight sheet metal.

24. This 1946 Pontiac Torpedo sedan coupe is an eight-cylinder one. Note the small badge at the front of the front fender spears. Only eight-cylinder-powered Ponchos had them.

25. Two late '40s Hudson step-down models sit a few rows from the front.

26. Kaiser-Frazer fans figure this foursome of two Kaisers and two Frazers is from the '50s.

27. A pair of "Ply Mouths" hunkers in the weeds. Both the '41 (at left) and the '40 (at right) show signs of some nasty encounters, but both are 85-90 percent complete.

28. Stout bumpers and other robust mechanical features made the Checker cars almost indestructible and likely candidates for taxicabs. This one is from the early '60s.

29. This 1946 Ford Railroad Delivery truck would make a dandy camper for someone with a little money, a bunch of ingenuity, lots of time on his hands and a craving for an ice breaker to start idle conversations.

30. Sonny Clinkscales, owner of Clinkscales, is an avid collector in his own right. One of his favorites is a '47 Ford 1-1/2 tonner that he shows regularly. It won its Junior First at the AACA nationals held in Greenville, S.C.

31. Also from Sonny's private collection is a 1935 Ford with dump bed. Last plated in 1941, it showed only 41,000 original miles when Sonny found it in New York and brought it home to South Carolina. It runs and is slated for a complete restoration.

32. Another car from the collection is this 1947 Chevrolet convertible, which has been gone through from top to bottom. It sports a fresh maroon paint job.

**1.** Hugh L. Hodges, Jr. and Sr. grew up on the family farm that has been in the family for several generations. It was here that the salvage business was started and remains. H.L. Hodges Sr. retired a few years ago.

## Seldom visited by old car and truck collectors, this is one yard that has not been picked over

Photos by the author

# H.L. Hodges Salvage Yard & Used Parts

## Monroe, Georgia

**2.** The aisles are mowed but tall weeds are around most cars. Here's a 1960 Oldsmobile two-door hardtop that has many parts to offer.

by Ken New

Hugh L. Hodges, Jr. operates one of those salvage yards you only hear about by word of mouth. In this case, word of mouth has a '90s twist in the form of an electronic page on the worldwide web. It's the pet project of 27-year-old Doug Aherns, Athens, Geo., a State of Georgia Board of Regents systems support employee who is a computer guy and an old car enthusiast. The web page is a growing list of obscure salvage yards that Aherns has visited, photographed and posted on the internet. Aherns graciously offered to lead us to several of these yards within a 50-mile radius of the Atlanta and Athens area. Hodges is one of those yards.

Hodges is located in rural Georgia near Monroe and that's where the contact with the nineties seems to fade quickly. A throw-back to the old days when individuals parted out cars to keep their personal cars rolling, this salvage yard has

3. This '50 Merc four-door with its distinctive rear suicide doors has not been stripped as clean as expected. Old Merc taillights and trim are big buck items.

4. Most of the vehicles at Hodges aren't parted out extensively. This once handsome mid-'50s GMC has a Hydra-Matic transmission and step-side bed.

5. The basic good looks of the famed Loewy-designed coupe is pleasing even after the ravages of nature have reduced this '54 Studebaker coupe to a crinoline reminder of its former grace.

few of the modern conveniences of a well financed salvage operation, save for a phone. There are lots of briars and weeds so pack your boots and long pants. But it's worth it as this salvage yard has cars – some 1200 to 1,500 of them ranging from the '40s into the '70s – and most aren't picked clean of usable parts.

H.L. Hodges' salvage endeavors were unceremoniously started in the early 1950s when H.L. Hodges, Sr. began dragging cars home to the family farm where the operation began and still resides. H.L. Hodges, Jr., the current owner, was born there and it seemed only natural for him to fall into his father's footsteps. H.L. Jr. maintains the work ethic as well. At times, you'll find him single-handedly taking care of customers and putting in long hours six days

a week – even on Sunday sometimes. Hodges says he isn't normally open on Sunday, but since he lives just down the road and "I'm usually around on Sundays. Just call ahead."

Customers can pull their own parts as long as no safety issues are present, i.e. don't crawl under a car with a bumper jack holding it up. Oh, and bring your own tools. ∎

## ABOUT THE YARD

H.L. Hodges Salvage Yard & Used Parts, Inc., 3995 Treadwell Bridge Rd., Monroe, GA 30656, phone 770-267-3461 is owned and operated by Hugh L. Hodges, Jr. Business hours are 9 a.m. to 4 p.m., Monday through Friday, and 9 a.m. to 4 p.m., Saturday. H.L lives just down the road and doesn't mind an occasional Sunday visitor. The yard is located roughly midway between Atlanta and Athens, Ga. From I-85 take Hwy. 316 east to US 78. Turn west toward Monroe. Cross the Apalachee River and turn right on the second road (Bradley Gin Rd.). Hodges is located one mile ahead on the right.

6. Stripped of its trim and trappings, this '55 Chevrolet Bel Air hardtop has been in the yard for several years.

7. King of the popular demolition derby cars, the Chrysler Imperial built in the early '60s was almost indestructible due to its rigid frame construction. However, this '61 has escaped combat. The body remains straight and true — so does the frame.

8. With Ford's first-ever wraparound windshield on a production pickup truck, there's no doubt this is a 1956 F-100.

9. A 1967 first-year Pontiac Firebird at Hodges is equipped with a 326 with two-barrel and other niceties, such as a vinyl top.

10

10. There are barely enough features visible through the grasses to identify this 1941 Ford Special DeLuxe.

11. Sprawled out on the ground, this '59 Rambler four-door is fairly complete, but it shows signs of gross neglect.

12. Cute little VW Beetle from the late '60s peeks through the grass. Hodges has a number of VW products, including vans.

11

12

13

13. Six Olds models were built in the Dynamic 88 line in 1964. This sporty two-door hardtop has given up the ghost but not all of its parts.

14

15

16

17

18

19

14. 1963 Chevrolet Fleetside pickups with short beds are real popular in the southeastern part of the country. The Fleetside cost $16 more than the Stepside cousin in '63.

15. This 1972 MG Midget has given up its taillights and backup lights but the desirable wire wheels are still bolted on.

16. Lettered mid-'60s White heavyweight 10-wheeler has gone unmolested since it retired to Hodges from the ready-mix concrete business.

17. Rough and ready posture of this 1974 International six-wheeler is alluring to truck enthusiasts.

18. Attracting lots of customers to Ford in '62 were the Town Sedan models, four-door models that defy the notion that four-door models are stodgy by nature.

19. Popular with practical people, the '63 Ford Falcon was a real workhorse that demanded little attention or gasoline.

20

21

22

23

24

25

20. In 1954 Ford dropped the venerable flathead engine in favor of an overhead valve design. A Crestline four-door with an ohv V-8 waits out its fate at Hodges.

21. An integral cab/box Ford half-ton from 1961 is decked out with aftermarket wheels and tires. It's weathered but virtually complete.

22. Discarded transmissions surround this white '63 Ford Fairlane 500 hardtop. Steel roof simulates the contours of a convertible.

23. An unknown driver named Bobby piloted this first generation Mustang, old 79, in dirt track action. It is fitted with roll bars and a wide differential.

24. All 1969 Cadillacs were powered by a 472-cid V-8 that produced 375 horses, including this Coupe de Ville.

25. A Jeep dating to the early '40s has military written all over it. Note the sunken headlamps and no tailgate. Beefy bumper and tow bar are add-ons.

Photos by the author

1. This Mercury station wagon represents the most expensive and weighty Merc in 1954. It was positioned in the top of the line Monterey series in '54, having been shifted up from the lower Custom line in 1953.

# Collins Auto Salvage, Inc.

## Auburn, Georgia

## "Never scrap the oldies" policy means there's always vintage tin here

2. Outdoor photographers loved the 1963 Studebaker Wagonaire station wagon, which featured a rear gate with retracting glass and a sliding roof. Thus, shooting on the move with a camera on a tripod sitting inside the wagon's rear compartment was a snap.

Gerald Collins has salvaged thousands of cars since 1969, when he realized that selling old car parts was a more lucrative business than building houses and painting cars on the side. Although success for the owner of a salvage yard that contains more than 3,000 cars didn't happen overnight, Collins jokingly indicated he was a bit trapped in his success, having "gotten into it and discovering he couldn't get out." According to Collins, he "worked in a yard as a kid and fooled around with old cars," then got back into it when his home building business soured. He has been at the same location since day one.

Collins Auto Salvage maintains an inventory of 500-1000 older cars corralled at the back of its 25-acre yard. The older stock is out of the flow of daily business, yet easily accessible to old car owners who wish to remove their own parts. Customers are allowed to remove parts, but the line is drawn when removing those parts involving raising the car and crawling underneath. Collins sends one of his fork lift operators to handle such jobs due to the risk of injury. Customers who are unable to remove their own

3. Varying shades of fading paint on the left rear quarter of this Olds show the outlines of the eagle's beak exterior trim, used on the 88s in 1955.

4. Formerly yellow and now red, this 1966 Dodge Coronet hardtop has been stripped of its brightwork, while the basic structure remains intact.

5. Although not seen very well from this angle, the short top that Ford fitted to its shoebox coupes in '49 made it the most attractive one in the line. Shown here is a 1950 coupe.

## ABOUT THE YARD

Collins Auto Salvage, Inc., 574 Blackstock Rd., Auburn, GA 30011, phone 770-963-2650, is owned and operated by Gerald Collins. Business hours are 8 a.m. to 6 p.m. Monday through Thursday, 8 a.m. to 5 p.m. on Friday, and 8 a.m. to 4 p.m. on Saturday. Collins Auto Salvage, Inc. is located northeast of Atlanta, Ga. within 3 miles of I-85. Take the Hamilton Mill exit from I-85 and travel south to Georgia Hwy. 124. Turn left onto 124 and proceed to Mt. Mariah Rd. At the 4-way stop, look for Collins' sign on the left.

6

6. Frazer didn't offer a pickup truck in the late '40s, but later in the car's life someone thought it might be a good idea. The bed appears to be Ford.

7. A 1966 Plymouth Fury III hardtop could be ordered with either a six or eight-cylinder engine. Production amounted to 41,869 units.

8. The sturdy bumper on this 1956 Pontiac four-door has the optional front bumper Master Grille Guard still in place.

9. Another converted pickup sedan at Collins is a 1941 Ford that was chopped in half just behind the front seat and crudely fitted with sheet metal to keep the rain out.

7

8

9

parts due to various reasons can arrange for parts removal by one of Collins' yard men and shipment via UPS or truck. Collins sells parts and complete cars.

From our travels around Georgia, we found that the clay soil and mild climate are conducive to only moderate rusting of car bodies. This part of the country has a wealth of restorable parts waiting to be harvested. ∎

10

11

10. It's unusual to see a retired '53 Chevy with its original toothy grille. Very popular with customizers in the late '50s and '60s, the grilles were bolted inside a myriad of open mouths.

11. Buick's most popular seller in 1960 was the LeSabre four-door. Surface rust aside, this old Flint filly is fairly complete and willing to share parts.

12. The serial number on this '65 Ford Galaxie 500 two-door fastback indicates it retired near its birthplace – the Atlanta Ford assembly plant.

12

13

13. A more popular model in this condition may never have arrived at Collins Salvage. Certainly, this '65 Pontiac Bonneville wouldn't have sat very long before a collector carted it away.

14. Doug Ahern, Athens, Ga. has a soft spot for Mopars. Here Ahern examines a 1973 Plymouth Gold Duster wearing its original black canopy roof vinyl top in a golden reptile pattern, but void of its exterior graphics package. There are signs of a major side swipe to the driver's side of the car.

14

15

15. Like many family members in the 1951 Hudson Pacemaker line, this four-door was fitted with four bumper guards; the outside two were optional. Only two of the four remain.

16

16. Straight and shiny, the front chrome is above average on this 1956 Buick Special four-door, Model 41. A few other pieces of exterior trim are long gone.

17. Shabby and abandoned in despair, this '55 Olds was a potent puppy when it hit the streets with a four barrel carb-equipped Rocket 88 engine.

18. Station wagons offered by Ford in 1955 wore larger tires than the others. Non-wagons wore 6.70 x 15s and the wagons 7.10 x 15s, but you'd never know it by looking at this barefoot Country Sedan.

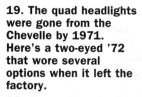

19. The quad headlights were gone from the Chevelle by 1971. Here's a two-eyed '72 that wore several options when it left the factory.

20. About the only sign of abuse this '62 Chevy Bel Air doesn't wear is rust.

21

21. From this tag team of '58 Buicks, a restorer could rescue almost enough parts to put together a respectable vehicle.

22. The sheet metal is pretty good and the glass is good on this '71 Buick Riviera.

23. A Willys pickup built in the early '50s is kind of cute even in this disheveled condition.

24. She's not rusty, but most major body parts are beat up. Only the driver's door of this '68 Olds Cutlass is straight.

22

23

24

25. Patriotic '57 Chevy hardtop started out white, was painted blue and then red before it ended up at Collins. Paint code is 794 for Imperial Ivory.

26. Although built by the thousands in the 1960s, you rarely see a Ford Econoline restored.

27. 1954 Ford F-100 pickup has been swatted in the front, but from the doors on back, the sheet metal is salvageable.

28. White on the outside and red on the inside was a very popular combination with Ford buyers in 1963.

29. Here's a two toned red and white 1956 Oldsmobile 88 two-door. The headlamps are gone but not the distinctive hood trim.

Photos by the author

1. Owen Weatherley is still going strong as he nears his 80th birthday. Weatherley says he "doesn't have anything in the yard that doesn't have a radiator."

by Ken New

**W**eatherley Old Cars & Parts, Winder, Ga. is officially open for business on Saturday only. But owner Owen Weatherley, a stout and resourceful gentleman nearing 80, says he doesn't venture far and you can usually catch him by phone during the week.

When Saturday comes, you'll find Weatherley pacing about his driveway, chatting with customers. In his part of Georgia, the winters are mild and scrounging for parts even during the summers is pleasant since the salvage yard is located in a thick woods behind

# Weatherley's Old Cars & Parts

## Winder, Georgia

2. Standing near the modest sign that marks the entrance to Weatherley's Old Cars & Parts is Doug Ahern, a 27-year-old member of the Georgia Board of Regents' systems support team, i.e. a computer whiz. Ahern maintains a junkyard web page on the internet. Ahern says he was disappointed that no pictures, etc. of old cars were on the 'net, so he began to photograph obscure salvage yards near his home in Athens, Ga., then post them on the Internet. Weatherley's is one of those yards.

3. Weatherley's daily driver is a 1952 IH pickup. He drives it back and forth in his driveway to flatten aluminum soda cans.

# Georgia pines and cudzu harbor 150-200 old cars

Weatherley's house. At the back of Weatherley's driveway, a narrow path flanked on both sides by shoulder-high rows of car parts snakes into the thicket where the cars are found.

There are discarded brake rotors, hubcaps, shocks and every imagineable type of car part. Most were well worn and likely unusable, but there's something magical about the helter skelter way they were flipped aside. The urge to turn over every hubcap and rusty part was almost irresistible. Weatherley's collection of cars is less accessible due to the thick underbrush ahead.

The collection of 150-200 cars is located up the winding path scattered among rapidly growing pine trees and cudzu that has gotten a little out of hand since Weatherley closed his repair garage and retired some 15 years ago. You can't see the repair garage either, although it's located off to the left only 25 yards from the driveway.

Weatherley took a moment to explain his sales policy. "I was born just before the Depression hit. Worked hard all my life and don't believe in welfare. I don't

4

5

6

4. The "Trail of Tears" leads from Weatherley's front yard into an aggressive grove of pines and cudzu where some 300 cars dwell in relative privacy.

5. A remnant of 25 years ago when Weatherley quit his job at GM in Doraville and started fixing cars full time, this weathered sign hangs in a garage at the end of the Trail of Tears.

6. There's a lot of parts hanging around here. It's doubtful if Weatherley ever threw anything away. He doesn't work in the garage anymore, but just stores more stuff in it.

have any cars that have a radiator. I don't do mail orders. You remove your own parts around here and pay on the way out. I don't want to get rich – just want to get a fair price."

And, like a lot of other resourceful folk who remember the difficult days of the Depression, Weatherley threw nothing away that he felt might be useful sometime in the future. Most of his cars are reasonably complete and offer good pickings for restorers. Admittedly, the dampness, and heavy insulation of felled leaves and pine needles have taken a toll, but Weatherley says he drove every one of these cars before they were dragged into his yard. Many, he vows, would probably start with a freshly charged battery and a little gas. ■

7. Bashed Nash? No! Actually, the rotund '55 is rather straight albeit covered with pine needles as is every car in this collection of homeless and needy veterans.

8. Hiding out in this grove of pine trees, this '48 Chevy Fleetline has kept its trim pieces. The cars are not picked clean of desirable parts.

9. Once loved or hated for its exciting stealth-like styling, the '57 Plymouth Belvedere stirs emotions even today.

10. A pair of medium-priced jewels, a '57 Merc sedan and a '58 Pontiac two-door hardtop, are located on a bank that runs through Weatherley's property.

11. Out behind the garage, one finds row after row of abandoned cars. Weatherley says he drove each and every one of his cars into the yard.

12. Waiting for the cudzu to envelope it during the approaching summer months, this bullet-nose Studebaker hails from the late '40s to early '50s.

13. 1955 Buick points its dagmars to a time when most GM cars sported a "damn good set of headlights."

14

15

14. It's no wonder why a number of buyers fell for the Bel Air four-door hardtop in turquoise and white in '57.

15. Desirable 1968 Dodge Dart GTS dominated the Dart pack with its rear bumble bee stripes and fancy but non-functioning hood scoops. It's pretty obvious this unflowered one came to a sudden stop before relegated to Weatherley's orphan's home.

16. Studebaker celebrated its 100th year in 1952. Work on a new body design didn't make it in time for the centennial.

17. The round shapes at the tops of the roof and fenders and the flat sides made the '57 Buick line look as heavy as a tank. This one is a Special.

16

17

18

19

18. Mopar, Chevy, Ford, and Ford. The lines stretch into the hundreds among the pines and cudzu which, fortunately, was in its dormant season during our visit.

19. The rear section of this 1960 Cadillac doesn't reveal why it ended up at Weatherleys.

20. The through-the-bumper exhaust design flowered in the mid-50s. Here a '56 Ford Town Sedan illustrates the better idea from Ford that made for smokey bumper ends on poor running cars.

20

21. Nosing into the pine needles is an early '50 Cadillac two-door hardtop that appears in pretty decent shape despite its dismal fate.

22. Lever-type exterior door handles were seen on the Mercury for the last time in 1949 and replaced with pushbuttons in '50.

23. Weatherley's Reo wrecker with its homemade boom would probably start with a fresh battery, according to its owner. Superfluous sheet metal was abandoned during the conversion. Pay close attention and you can pick out a tired Doug Aherns resting on another skidder to the left.

Photos by the author

1. One of the driving forces behind "Texas Exports" Little Valley Auto Ranch is Danny Barkley, a 46-year-old Hoosier transported to Texas in 1968 by his father, Charles, a career military man stationed at Ft. Hood. The 1960 Ford panel truck was purchased by the pair more than 30 years ago. It is powered by a 350 Chevy engine.

2. "Texas Exports" Little Valley Auto Ranch's owners don't stay at home waiting for customers. Annually, they transport vehicles to 40 swap meets around the country. This threesome headed for a meet in Arlington, Texas included a 1971 Chevy Cheyenne pickup with mostly original paint and in drive-home condition, a '57 Chevy Bel Air two-door hardtop with V-8 and auto, and an X11 code RS SS '69 Camaro convertible in white. The unrestored underside of the Camaro was amazingly clean and showed bright factory black paint. The front end had some collision damage.

# "Texas Exports" Little Valley Auto Ranch

## Belton, Texas

# Old folks home where senior Texas cars, especially mid-'50s Chevys, wait for adoption

by Ken New

"Texas Exports" Little Valley Auto Ranch is located in dry, south central Texas where automobiles approach old age gracefully without serious challenges from rust and corrosion. Fortunately for restorers and collectors of vintage cars from other parts of the country where Mother Nature isn't so kind to aging automobiles, enterprising brothers Danny and Mike Barkley have corraled a large number of these well-preserved seniors and offer them to collector car enthusiasts. From its Belton, Texas site, "Texas Exports" Little Valley Auto Ranch tenders a herd of more than 600 hand-picked vintage cars, including some 75 Chevys from 1955-57, from which thousands of rare parts can be salvaged and a number of "project cars" can be recycled into the collector car arena.

The Barkleys describe their "project cars" as vehicles that may show some wear and tear but are basically complete and need only moderate refurbishment

3. Mike Barkley (left) serves as the office manager and takes care of shipping chores. Brother Danny (right) started the business in 1981. He says he has never tired of tracking down interesting cars and doing swap meets. This pair has placed hundreds of quality project cars in the hands of collectors – mostly Midwesterners.

4. One of the more interesting cars at "Texas Exports" Little Valley Auto Ranch is this '56 Chevy two-door hardtop. It was built in the Oakland, Calif. plant and has a VC code, which tells us it is a V-8 from the Bel Air line.

## ABOUT THE YARD

"Texas Exports" Little Valley Auto Ranch, Rt. 7, Box 7085, Belton, TX 76513, (corner of Wheat Rd. & Hwy. 190), phone 254-939-8548 or cell phone 254-760-7431, is owned and operated by brothers Danny and Mike Barkley. Danny stocks the yard and Mike manages the office. "Texas Exports" Little Valley Auto Ranch operates a salvage yard, sponsors four editions of "Texas Swap Meet" per year, and sets up at some 40 swap meets each season. Quality project cars and individual parts are the specialties of this business. Belton, Tex. is located some 120 miles south of Dallas/Fort Worth, Texas. From I-35, take exit 293A and drive one mile to the Loop 121 exit. Take the service road (it runs parallel to the Interstate highway) for one mile to "Texas Exports" Little Valley Auto Ranch, which will be on the right. Weekday business hours are 9:30 a.m. to 5:30 p.m. (CST). Saturday hours are 9:30 a.m. to 4 p.m. Closed on Sunday. Delivery of parts and complete cars is available. Call for details.

5.

5. There are around 600 cars at the Belton, Tex. location. Almost all are from that part of the country. That means skin cancer has rarely eaten deeply into the bodies. A '49 Pontiac Silver Streak four-door and a '57 Nash Ambassador Super are excellent examples of cars that have never been touched.

6. The Buick Riviera was restyled in 1966. Here's a nice one ready for restoration. The headlights were concealed by parts of the grille when not in use.

7. A 1964 Pontiac convertible has solid sheet metal that needs some straightening, as well as doses of devotion and financial investment, to see it rejuvenated.

8. Red. Straight. Dry. Available. Waiting for a buyer. For a T-Bird fancier, this 1963 Ford Thunderbird coupe is about as nice a project car as one could want.

6.

7.

8.

to return them to their glory days.

Danny Barkley, president and "head scrounger," says Little Valley tries to work with buyers to find just the right car to begin a restoration project. Often, he and brother Mike will hold a car for a while to give themselves time to find and replace missing or damaged parts. Sometimes, a straight door is needed or maybe a decent front fender, etc. Danny Barkley says that "by offering project cars that don't need a lot of restoration, we do many restorers a favor," especially first-time restorers and those without restoration skills or imagination.

Danny Barkley says he and his brother have witnessed situations where wives of prospective buyers have frowned on purchases simply because they couldn't see the potential in a less-than-perfect car.

"All they see is a pile of worthless parts," Barkley says. Often, by painting a car, fitting a grille into an opening, etc., the marital pains of adopting a restoration project that will require a substantial commitment of time and money are eased considerably. "We have sold hundreds of project cars since the business was started in 1981. Especially in the Midwest," he added. Judging from the customers who have returned numerous times to this reputable old car adoption agency, "Texas Exports" Little Valley Auto Ranch appears to be performing a much needed service.

If you are the least bit curious about how "Texas Exports" Little Valley Auto Ranch got its name, you'll appreciate how Danny Barkley, sitting in front of his television set in 1981, arrived at what we consider to be the perfect name. The name "Texas Exports" Little Valley Auto Ranch is a spoof directed at the popular 1980s TV series "Dallas." You may recall a family named Barkleys – J. R. was the ramrod. The Barkleys rode herd over a vast empire of oil and land holdings from the Big Valley Ranch. It seemed only natural to Danny Barkley that he, a Barkley with a "little" business from a "little" spread in Belton, should name his business Little Valley Auto Ranch. ("Texas Exports" was added five years ago to serve a broader business plan.) Some 20 years later, we find it amusing that the significance of the ranch that was a pictorial stand-in for the imaginary Big Valley Ranch has dwindled to a designated bus stop for retirees, while the real-life Barkley's spread, "Texas Exports" Little Valley Auto Ranch, has become synonymous with quality restorable old cars and parts. ∎

9. 1960 Chevrolet El Camino is as solid as a jug. Most of the doghouse sheet metal is stowed in the bed.

10. This is not a real convertible. It's a salad bar. This '57 Chevrolet awaits delivery to a New York restaurant owner who purchased the car and had its top cut off. It will be the center attraction in a food serving arrangement.

11

11. The engine and suspension are gone from this '56 Chevy 150 two-door post sedan. The sheet metal is pretty nice.

12. Straight as an arrow and with no rust, this '55 Chevy doghouse will be sold as is or will be joined with other parts to become a project car that the Barkleys will resell.

13. With fresh paint and a few other improvements, this green 1961 Chevrolet Impala hardtop would be ready to enjoy.

14. Excellent '58 Chevy pickup body has all of the requirements one would want for a ground-up restoration project.

12

13

14

15

16

15. A pair of friendly '54 Chevrolets awaits adoption. Both the hardtop, at left, and the two-door post have great potential.

16. This 1948 Chrysler coupe has a solid floor pan, dry sheet metal and restorable brightwork.

17. Another pickup cab that would be a great one with which to begin a project is this '55 GMC.

18. A handsome design that wears well is exemplified by this 1974 Nova Spirit of America edition. It has its original 81,000-mile motor.

17

18

19

19. Danny Barkley says this '47 Packard limo is so long it hangs off both ends of his 18-foot trailer. The motor was rebuilt in the '70s.

20. Starting with a sloped-back '51 Chevy, an unknown body man built this custom. It has '53 fenders and hood up front and '53 fenders and '54 taillights at the rear. The workmanship is excellent.

21. 1953 was a great year to love Buicks. Buick celebrated its 50th anniversary by introducing the V-8 engine in all of its lines except the Special; 55 percent of Buick customers opted for V-8-powered cars. Here's a nice two-door hardtop Special.

22. About as crisp as they come, this clean-bodied 1955 Ford was once owned by a college professor who taught body work at Central Texas College. It was refreshed for shop credits by his students.

20

21

22

23. Barkley found this '55 Chevy two door at Ft. Hood in nearby Waco, Tex. The trim number is 500 and the paint number is 587. Translated, it means this baby was sprayed Neptune Green and was trimmed in gray cloth.

24. This 1959 Ford station wagon has a 352 motor, air and a padded dash. It is ready to drive away.

25. This 1974 Dodge Challenger with slap stick and 383 was probably a 318 or 340 car originally. It's beautiful.

26. The Scott and White Hospital, which is located about 20 miles from Little Valley, used this '55 Ford cabover until just a few years ago. It would make a dandy car hauler. It has a clean Texas title.

**27.** Here's an unusual combination – a '54 Mercury with a 389 Pontiac under the hood. The body is real nice and hides nothing.

**28.** A straighter body you won't find anywhere. This '56 Chevy wagon has a couple of nice surprises. It came from the factory in red and white and equipped with air conditioning.

**29.** The lineage of this '55 Chevy makes it very interesting to '55 fans. It's a Gypsy Red and Ivory White (code 617) Del Ray complete with the quilted door panels. This California-built survivor was last plated in 1974.

30. The resourceful former owner of this '57 Buick converted it into a pickup. The paint is weathered, but the body underneath is solid and straight.

31. The Barkleys are '55 fans. Danny Barkley's high-school-age son, Dee, restored this '55 for his daily driver. It has a great sounding engine.

32. There weren't enough Hudsons around in '57 for the American public to ever get used to the distinctive look. This '57 has the V-8 motor.

33. Good replacement parts abound at "Texas Exports" Little Valley Auto Ranch. Among this array of goodies near the fence were doors for a '37 Chevy and a '68 Camaro, rear fenders for a '40 Ford, a '39 Ford Deluxe hood, '53-55 F100 doors and a '36 Ford coupe door, as well as other choice sheet metal.

34. Cab for a '49-53 Chevy pickup is definitely a take home and love item. It is solid and has opera windows.

35. With this photo, we enter the back part of "Texas Exports" Little Valley's salvage yard where the parts cars are stored. The south central section of Texas is kind to automobiles. Here, Mother Nature grants long lives to the bodies.

36. Still more of the parts cars that reside at "Texas Exports" Little Valley. The cars and trucks have all been selectively bought, then brought to the holding pen near Highway 190 since 1983.

37. Here you can see a '54 Merc, an old Corvair, a Jeep wagon, a Hudson, a Pontiac Firebird and others. The condition of the sheet metal is the fodder of legends in other parts of the country.

38. The author couldn't pass the chance to purchase the door on this '56 Ford F-100. Mike Barkley arranged for shipment of the part to Ohio where it will mate with his in-process '56. The door arrived nicely, wrapped in heavy cardboard with all the accompanying hardware carefully stowed inside.

39. Proud old '40 Ford two-door sedan hasn't given up the ghost yet. It waits for someone to breathe new life into her.

40. Old car builders who dream of grand projects love "Texas Exports" Little Valley. Here's a 1966 Dodge Charger in dark blue that spurs the imagination. Dig those flames!

41. Danny Barkley relayed the story of how this once pristine '56 Chevy Nomad came to be at "Texas Exports" Little Valley. Barkley says, "The former owner stored it in a barn for many years. Then one day along comes this school bus. It lost a wheel, ran off the road and into the barn where it demolished the Nomad."

42. Imagine what you could do with this '55 Chevy hardtop body. We've seen worse on the highway. "Texas Exports"Little Valley Auto Ranch has 80 '55-57 Chevys in stock. Their conditions vary.

43. Last plated in 1974, this '68-69 Ford Torino fastback still wears what appears to be original paint.

44. One of the author's favorites is the '55 Oldsmobile 88 hardtop. With a little gas and some luck, it might be made to run. The ground-up restoration it deserves would take a bit longer.

45. The author's wife, Judy, is a real champ. She willingly took notes as the photos were shot. She's also an animal lover who threatened a walk-out if she wasn't given time off to make friends with Prince, the local junkyard dog, in residence at "Texas Exports" Little Valley. Danny Barkley consoled the big bubbly, puppy dog as Judy searched for a spot to lay down her note pad. The grille of a '58 Edsel wagon can be seen at left.

46. With donations from a decent parts car, this '59 Chevy Impala hardtop could be restored.

# CTC Auto Ranch

## Sanger, Texas

Photos by the author unless otherwise noted

1. Seen from the access road that parallels I-35, CTC Auto Ranch, Sanger, Texas, is quite impressive.

## Texas-size holding of old cars and parts is a sight to behold

2. Brothers Allen (left) and David Williamson own and operate CTC Auto Ranch, Sanger, Tex. There are more than 2,600 cars on the 28-acre ranch/auto salvage yard. (Randoll Reagan photo)

by Ken New

If you share our passion for old cars and your heart stutters at the sight of rust-free old cars, be advised that you may not be prepared for the likes of CTC Auto Ranch. CTC is located about 20 miles north of Dallas, Texas. As we spied CTC from the big I-35 slab, we would have found it impossible to resist the urge to duck off the Interstate and spend a couple hours milling about the 2,600 cars on hand — even though we had made an appointment with David Williamson due to the efforts of Randoll Reagan, a greater Dallas resident who bird dogs salvage holdings for us in his part of the country.

As we dropped off the Interstate and craned our necks along the fence line leading up to CTC's main gate, we drove past several hundred vehicles that quickened our pulse like a buzz-saw. If you are fortunate to visit CTC, as we did, and start thinking this may be one of the most impressive hoards of old cars you've ever seen, you won't be without company. We've heard that many old car owners have shared your thoughts.

Run by amiable brothers, David and Allen Williamson with a little hands-on guidance from their semi-retired father

## ABOUT THE YARD

CTC Auto Ranch, 3077 Memory Lane, Sanger, TX 76266-7329, phone 940-482-3007 or 1-800-482-6199, FAX 940-482-3010, is is owned and operated by David, Allen and Dale Williamson. CTC Auto Ranch is located alongside I-35 some 20 miles North of Dallas, Texas. Take exit 474 from I-35, then drive North along the service road (running parallel with the Interstate highway) for about 1/4 mile to Memory Lane. Customers are not allowed to pull parts. CTC ships parts daily to faraway places. Weekday business hours are 8:30 a.m. to 5:30 p.m. (CST). Saturday hours are 9:00 a.m. to 1:00 p.m. Closed on Sunday.

3. Shelby Boren, left, is the sales clerk at CTC Auto Ranch. Part-owner David Williams usually takes all calls regarding vintage cars and parts. David is in charge of the Sanger, Tex. yard while his brother Allen travels within a 150-mile radius of the yard to purchase new inventory.

Dale, CTC Auto Ranch is about as close to automotive nirvana as we've ever experienced. At CTC we found tons and tons of prime vintage automotive sheet metal and trim parts and row after row of able-bodied cars that begged us to take them home.

One thing we didn't find much of at CTC Auto Ranch was rust-out – that disease that permeates cars from wetter climes. Rust is almost nonexistent around this dry part of Texas. In fact, it's rumored that the use of the word rust-out rarely enters into the conversations of local residents, that is, unless they are conversing about other parts of the country. If you take a close look at the cars they've driven and relegated to salvage yards such as CTC, you'll understand why the rust is considered to be nothing more than a thin orangy dust that shows up on sheetmetal after a lifetime or two.

CTC Auto Ranch has the look of a yard

4. The dry terrain is conducive to the storage of older cars. The rows of cars are orderly with wide aisles for access and removal of vehicles. CTC faces I-35 and is located a half-hour's drive north of Dallas, Tex. Some 2,600 vehicles are in stock. (Randoll Reagan photo)

5. CTC has a nice variety of Mopars in stock. This photo along the fence is representative of the condition of the cars. That's Interstate 35 in the distance. (Randoll Reagan photo)

6-8. The office walls and ceiling are covered with a pretty nice assortment of parts, including grilles, trim, hubcaps, splash shields, etc.

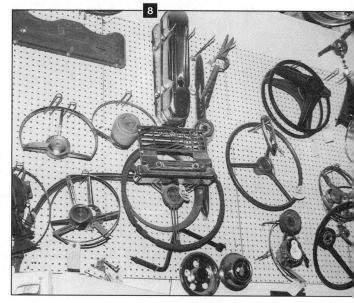

that's been around for many years, albeit better groomed than some of the oldies. But it isn't an oldie, at all. It wasn't around during WW II, has only heard of Elvis and Ralph Nader, and never experienced disco. In that regard, CTC is an infant having been in business since 1985. In 1990, it relocated to its current address which is within a stone's throw of I-35. Most cars date to the '50s and '60s with a few older ones scattered in the ranks. There's a respectable number from the 1970s.

A routine day at CTC finds David and Allen Williamson manning the phones, filling orders for rare parts, buying and selling cars or following up on leads to purchase a bunch of old cars to keep the 28-acre spread supplied with quality vintage cars and parts. David told *Cars & Parts* that "most of our cars come from within 150 miles of here," with CTC rarely getting cars from any place farther north than southern Oklahoma. The dealership decals I found on most trunk lids read like a local map. ∎

9. Just a short distance outside the front door of the office sits this one-owner '55 Chevy 210 with a 6-cylinder motor. It has a Powerglide trans and amazing sheet metal.

10. Willys wagons were perfect little vehicles to transverse the rolling range land around Sanger. These two 1952 models are looking for a new home.

11. Doesn't this beauty make your imagination soar? The brightwork on this '48 Pontiac Silver Streak went to a restorer in Hawaii and the fender somewhere else. The fender shield and under fender sheet metal are as dry as a powder horn.

12. A 1947 Cadillac hearse was traded to CTC by a street rodder who had planned to chop the top and update the drivetrain. It is very solid and straight.

13

13. Another AMC beauty is this '72 Javelin that appears to have its original paint, although somewhat faded, and most of its unique trim. AMC built some real lookers in the late '60s and early '70s. A Gremlin, a Rambler and several other AMC products sit in the background.

14. Black and white '56 Pontiac hails from San Antonio, Tex., several hundred miles away. David Williamson says that most of the inventory at CTC Auto Ranch comes from locales within a 100-mile radius of Sanger, Tex.

15. A bit stressed by the hot sun, but nonetheless well preserved, this '60 Pontiac convertible has given up a few choice parts, but others remain.

14

15

16

16. Another '60 Pontiac convertible sits a short distance away. Just think what you could do with both of them. At this point, it would be hard to decide which one would become the parts car. They are both pretty nice.

17. CTC has three Marlins. This '65 runs but suffers from a broken shift pin. This would be a great start for an AMC fan.

18. Guppy-eyed '59 Studebaker is an interesting study in how to prolong re-engineering the body. Studebaker Corp. was struggling during the period when this baby was born. Life in Texas has been kind to this South Bend, Ind. example.

19. This 1955 Studebaker Commander four-door two-toner is fairly complete except for its dental work, a headlamp and hubcaps.

20. Another 1955 Stude. This time, it's a hardtop Commander with a later model trunk lid.

21. A 1956 Clipper represents the lower line of cars from Packard. This four-door gave up its taillights to a customizer. Otherwise it appears to be complete.

22. A couple of early '60s Pontiac Bonneville convertibles, one on the ground with minor surface rust and dings and one on the truck bed showing a bit more damage. David Williams says any part from any car in his yard is for sale.

23. What better place to look for 1966 Ranchero parts than on a ranch. The Williamsons run as many as 30 head of longhorn cattle on their grounds to keep the grass down.

24. Unflappable and brash styling on this '59 Plymouth Savoy six-cylinder has stood the test of time very well.

25. It's too bad this photo doesn't show how rust-free this pile of dry Texas sheet metal really is. Outside storage in this dry terrain is not a threat to its quality.

26. The paint on this neglected Impala from '58 has seen better days. Not to worry – underneath the lousy paint, the body metal is solid and very salvageable.

27. The white body of this 1966 Plymouth Fury III hardtop shows no hints of rust.

28. A 1964 Chevy Malibu keeps company with a number of well-preserved GM products.

29. Green, green, rust unseen; a correct assessment of this 1956 Chevrolet two-door post sedan with gorgeous body panels.

30. This 1948 Chevrolet Fleetline Aero sedan has been picked over a bit but the major parts are still intact.

31. A pair of early '50s Chevys, a '51 at left and a '50 at right, sits butt to butt in this area which doubles as a place to store both cars and parts.

32. The Texas heat is tough on vinyl tops but kind to vintage tin. The rear quarters on this '71 Pontiac are solid.

33. Loyal trio of '57 Chevys stands ready to donate their ever-so-nice bodies and vital parts so another fellow five-seven can live.

34

34. It appears that a '59 Ford fancier bought the taillights and went his way. What remains is worthy of a similar fate.

35. Arriving from nearby Gainesville, Tex., just north of CTC Auto Ranch, this appealing '58 Ford Fairlane 500 hardtop is almost ready to drive away.

36. Several Edsels can be found directly behind the shop at CTC. All are fairly sound. This '59 Ranger stands at the end of a pack of four.

37. You'd have to travel quite a ways to find a drier '58 Edsel Ranger than this one at CTC Auto Ranch.

35

36

37

38. There weren't many Hudsons built in 1942. The two small trim pieces running from the grille onto the front fenders identify it as a '42. Actually there should be three pieces – the center one is missing.

39. Need a grille and front bumper for a '55 Merc? Here's a threesome, a red Monterey, a pink and white Montclair and a black Monterey that could supply a number of choice items.

40. The two-door Ford Ranch Wagon of 1956 was a workhorse with cargo space of 5 x 8 feet when the tailgate was lowered. Most of the plated trim has been stripped from this very nice body.

41. One of the more reserved members of the CTC family is this worldly 1950 Lincoln Cosmo. Its sleek lines are easy to take.

42. Did someone say Texas? A friend of the Williamson family loans about 20 head of longhorn cattle to CTC to keep the grass down and to discourage undesirable access to the yard at night. We almost came face to face with Mommy Longhorn who preferred to be left alone to munch as she pleased. We agreed. Her partner can be seen in the background.

43. Fair floor pans remain in this '47 Ford two-door sedan. Remaining body panels and assemblies are pretty decent as well.

44. David Williams says he bought this '55 Ford race car from an old boy who raced it in the '60s. The novel bumper is a real gem.

45. For those who look closely, a pair of longhorns can be seen grazing behind the pony cars representing the first and second generation Mustangs.

46

46. We liked the novel way the rear fenders extended from this '46 Ford half-ton. It appears to be very complete.

47. Here's a nice beginner car for just about anyone from teenager to retiree who has a passion for Mustangs and some time to spend on its restoration. It's a '68 with a six-banger. The missing parts are available from donor cars at CTC.

48. This is one of the few cars that CTC prefers to not part out. A second generation Camaro, it has lots of potential.

49. Cute little '70 Dodge Dart in purple with white stripe has a lot of appeal and some choice options. The Texas A&M stickers are a nice touch also.

47

48

49

50. This 1940 Ford Standard two-door sedan needs a little help, but it would be time well spent to bring her back.

51. A closeup of the '40 Dodge illustrates the manner in which sheet metal ages in south central Texas. It can have numerous scrapes and bruises, but it isn't heavily rusted.

52. Friendly '65 Plymouth Barracuda has V-8 power. Here's another nice starter car for a budding collector who wishes to turn a wrench or two.

53. One of the most interesting cars at CTC Auto Ranch for Studebaker fans, and maybe others, is this tri-tone 1955 Studebaker Speedster which has a plethora of options straight from the factory.

**54**

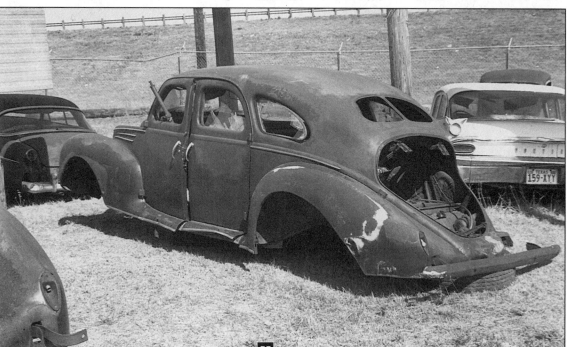

**55**

54-55. A pair of '39 Lincoln Zephyrs were brought to CTC Auto Ranch from Oklahoma by an enterprising trucker. Williams says either can be bought for around $1,000. We don't expect this pair to last very long.

56. CTC has a number of late '40s and early '50s F-1 Ford pickup projects. This string included half a dozen or so.

57. Strategically placed behind CTC billboard, this row of seductive beauties lures passers-by from I-35, a major highway that heads into Dallas, some 20 miles south. Included are '47 and '41 Buicks and a pair of Dodges, a '40 and a '39.

**56**

**57**

Photos by the author
except noted otherwise

1. The three Snyder brothers are Frank (left), Alan and Gene. They run a complete restoration service in addition to their salvage business. Frank and Alan are excellent mechanics and sheet metal men. Gene sets the shop's work schedule and handles all sales. (Snyder photo)

## The Snyder brothers have spent their lives around old cars

# Snyder Bros. Garage & Auto Wrecking

## Whitney, Texas

2. Even though the paved road stops a few hundred yards shy of Snyder Bros. Garage & Auto Wrecking in this remote part of Texas, customers from all over the land line up to bring their old cars to the Snyder brothers. They've been at this location since 1970.

by Ken New

Snyder Bros. Garage & Auto Wrecking, Whitney, Tex. is one of the older salvage operations profiled in this book. Brothers Gene, Alan and Frank Snyder were young boys when their father, Albert, got them started in the automotive repair business. Today, after a half century of working hand in hand, the Snyders are proof-positive that family members can perform top quality automotive restoration work, run a profitable salvage business and keep sibling rivalry in tow, especially when a dominant father figure steers the business course. Albert Snyder passed away 4-1/2 years ago, yet the Snyder brothers continue to dish out customer satisfaction in Texas-sized portions while broadening their reputation as Nash experts due in part to their fondness and admiration of the vehicles their father fostered for more than half a century. Among the 50 or so Nash cars that call Snyders home are vehicles in various states of repair. A favorite of the brothers is a 1938 Lafayette, a "baby Nash" that Gene Snyder has owned and driven since 1961.

Paying a visit to Snyder Bros. is like stepping back 30 years to the days when small family-run garages were common and salvage yards presented a rather disorganized appearance. Once you drop off Interstate 35, some 12-15 miles from Snyder's, the pace of life seems to slow down a bit. Nearing the end of your drive, the black top stops abruptly and turns into flying gravel. A quarter mile later, Snyder Bros. comes into view on your right. When pulling off the road, you'll find the front of Snyder Bros. Garage & Auto Wrecking's shop, unassuming and well worn, a business that exists solely on its hard-earned reputation. No sales person will greet you from behind a counter and you'll probably find the Snyders busy at work under the hood of a venerable oldie, or reshaping a stubborn chunk of automotive sheet metal.

Gene, the oldest of the three brothers, runs the shop's schedule and handles all sales. Alan and Frank perform most of the mechanical and cosmetic restoration work, and also fulfill parts orders for shipment to locales, both foreign and domestic. ∎

## ABOUT THE YARD

Snyder Bros. Garage & Auto Wrecking, Rt. 4, P.O. Box 25, Whitney, TX 76692, phone 254-582-9746, is owned and operated by Gene, Frank and Alan Snyder. Complete mechanical and restoration services are offered. Whitney, Tex. is located north of Waco. From I-35, take the Hillsboro exit (exit 364B) and drive West on Hwy. 22. Take a right at the 3rd traffic light (at Court House Square) in Whitney, then drive seven miles and take a right onto FM 3050. The Snyder Bros. shop and salvage yard are located four miles ahead. Notes: FM 3050 turns into a gravel road just before you get to Snyder's and FM means Farm & Market. Weekday hours are 8:00 a.m. to 5:00 p.m. (CST). Saturday hours are 8:00 a.m. to noon. Closed on Sunday. All parts are pulled for the customer.

3. The 1941 Ford fire truck seen here is owned by Dr. Marshal Lewin, Waco, Tex., who has decided to part with the pumper. Snyder's will handle its sale. When droughts plagued Texas, Dr. Lewin hauled water in the pumper from a lake near Paradise, Tex. to water his neighbors' lawns.

4. The cars are packed pretty tightly at Snyder's. The inventory is 98 percent U.S.-made cars. Several Mopar and GM vehicles are seen here.

5. Here's one that's rarely seen – a 1937 Lafayette four-door sedan, which appears to be mostly original. Somewhere along the line, it received sealed beam headlights and small park/turn lamps were bolted to the hood sides.

6. The charm of the shoebox Ford from 1950 isn't lost under a coat of dust and fading paint. The body has great potential for a variety of projects from stock to modified.

7. One of the older vehicles at Snyder Bros. Garage is this 1924 Dodge DB coupe. It hasn't been on the road in many years.

8. Almost hidden in the tall weeds is a 1956 Chrysler Windsor sedan that — like most of Snyder Bros.'s complete cars — is virtually rust-free and straight.

9. A Chevrolet Fleetmaster from 1947, with its dog house gone, sags a bit in the rear. The sheet metal wouldn't require a ton of work to prepare it for fresh paint.

10. A couple of Nashes back up a distinctive Kaiser Manhattan sedan. All three are mostly complete and restorable. A '22 Dodge frame and running gear sits on top of the middle Nash.

11. A handsome and dust covered 1937 LaSalle sits out along the gravel road. It appears to be at least 95 percent complete.

12. A 1937 Studebaker Dictator sedan has a few options, i.e. park lamps and sidemounted spare. The body is very solid and fairly rust-free.

13. The opportunity to restore a rarely seen 1950 Chrysler Windsor Newport pillarless hardtop is waiting at Snyder's. A wraparound, three-piece rear glass was used to define the rear roofline of this charming example.

14. The Snyder brothers share a foundness for Nash vehicles. This 1947 Nash coupe has an accessory sunvisor over the windshield that proved very popular when it rained at outdoor drive-in movies. Several late '40s Nashes call Snyder Bros. home.

15. Stripped of its brightwork, a 1939 Plymouth coupe wears a newer paint job and headlamps from an unknown donor. The original headlamps are squarish with rounded corners and fit flush with the contours of the fenders.

16. Probably an import to the Texas countryside (it has lower body rust), this outlandish '61 Imperial Southhampton stands out like a sore thumb among its conservative neighbors. Front end treatment is just as unusual as the rear appears here.

17. What badge this Plymouth wore in 1968 may be questioned by original-only fans. Snyder Bros. will upgrade this Satellite to a Road Runner.

18. An unmistakable AMC Marlin fastback from 1965 rests down by the house. It appears to be in pretty good shape.

19

19. The rust-free condition of the fenders and trunk lids seen here would make it worthwhile to root through this pile of Texas tin. But, beware of the ticks.

20. From this angle, it's tough to say if this is a 1949 or '50 Chevrolet Fleetline since we can't see the bumpers or ornaments. Gene Snyder says it's a '49.

21. Sitting sassy and out of reach, this '47 Nash 600 surveys the 300 or so cars at Snyder Bros.

20

21

22. Yes, it's a woodie, but it's not for sale. This 1947 Nash waits for the Snyder Bros. to clear out their work agenda, then the mechanics will be restored. The car was found behind a hotel by owner Ron Stein, Houston, Tex. in the early '80s.

23. Snyder Bros. is closing in on the finishing touches of a ground up restoration on this 1949 Olds 98 convertible, one of John Wright's cars. Wright has commissioned several restorations at Snyder Bros. The car came from dry Southwest Texas.

24. Another in-process restoration is this 1949 Ford F-1. Very little remains to finish up this beauty. John Wright, Bedford, Tex. owns the green pickup.

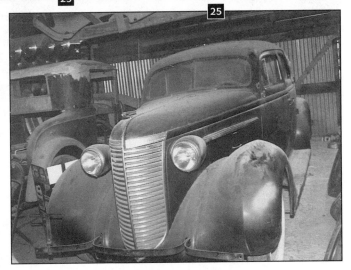

25. The trio of Snyder brothers knows Nash-built cars very well, having restored around 25-30 over the years. Gene has owned this 1938 Lafayette "Baby Nash" since 1961.

26

27

26-27. The marque of choice at this Texas hideout is Nash. There are some 50 Nashes in various states of repair at Snyder Bros., including big old sedans and cute little Metropolitans.

Photos by the author except as noted

1. Honest John's Caddy Corner, Justin, Tex. is located out of town a couple miles on a gentle hillside in an otherwise flat terrain. The facilities are relatively new and well equipped. Cadillac sales and parts sales are the cornerstone of the business. Some assembly and paint work is performed. The Cadillac sign once hung over Lone Star Cadillac in Dallas. Honest John worked at Lone Star before going to college where he majored in advertising. The white Caddy is a 1967 Coupe de Ville.

2. Cadillacs and Caddy parts line up alongside the lane leading up to Honest John's Caddy Corner. Most Cadillacs for sale are complete. Parts to make non-running Caddys roadworthy are available from Honest John's as well. (Randoll Reagan photo)

# Honest John's Caddy Corner

## A salvage business that caters to the Cadillac crowd

### Justin, Texas

by Ken New

3. Terrain not covered with cars is covered with Caddy parts – not an ideal place to run a lawn mower. (Randoll Reagan photo)

**H**onest John's Caddy Corner sits on a 10-acre plot just outside Justin, Tex. There on a slight hillside bulge in the otherwise flat rangeland, you'll find a collection of more than 300 Cadillacs corralled from points throughout the longhorn state. The Caddys are in various states of repair, ranging from those that need only charged batteries to make them roadworthy to listing hulks good for parts salvage only. Models from the late 1930s through the '80s are present.

Honest John's Caddy Corner represents a rather non-traditional method of marketing cars and parts to car restorers. By concentrating solely on the selling of Cadillacs and related parts, owner-operator John Foust has carved out one of the more distinct outlets for vintage cars and parts. If you need parts to restore or maintain your Cadillac, Foust believes it wise to go to a source where the proprietor knows Cadillacs. If you want parts for another brand of car, you'd better go somewhere else. It's that simple, says owner Foust, the 44-year-old Texan who rides herd on this unusual enterprise.

Foust says a fair amount of Honest John's Caddy Corner's business is done with people who maintain and restore Caddys from the late '60s and early '70s. Until recently Foust says he was "getting a lot of calls for 1959 and '60 convertible stuff but now the tide has turned to the newer, more affordable cars." There's also been "about a 20 percent increase in business" with folks who maintain daily drivers from the '80s. While walk-in traffic is a staple of Honest John's, Foust employs novel marketing methods to boost sales of vintage Cadillac parts.

Periodically, he sends mailings to current Cadillac dealers throughout the country. Usually, Cadillac dealers asked by their customers to service older Cadillacs find themselves without a viable source for obsolete parts, Foust says. "The mailings that have been ongoing for 10 years, now" have been a positive source of revenue by generating parts sales to the Caddy dealers or to the customer redirected to Honest John's Caddy Corner by the new car dealers.

Since many customers don't always know exactly what parts they need to make repairs, Foust also offers information to his customers from his vast Cadillac library, which includes original and reproduction workshop manuals, original owner's manuals, dealer albums and other reference books. Another interesting addition to Foust's sales arsenal has been an informative page on the worldwide web. The address is www.honestjohn.com.

Asked how he got hooked on Cadillacs, Foust confessed that Cadillac wasn't his first love back when he got his learners permit at the tender age of 15. He had his heart set on a sporty Mustang, but his father saw things a little differently and put him into a "Cadillac that had been

4. Honest John Foust (right) and Jimmy Broussard, a friend of John's from southern Louisiana. Foust and Broussard often team up when crunch time demands that a week's work be done in 24 hours. The pair poses at the side of the shop. Notice the rear of the sign spelling out Lone Star can be seen from this angle. At night the sign, done in turquoise neon, lights up the rural Texas skyline. Foust serves as one of the national directors of the Cadillac-LaSalle Club.

sitting around the house for two to three years." Foust says he was reluctant to drive the old white '60 sedan, but soon found out how much fun it was hauling around his friends.

In the spirit of the beat generation, he painted flowers and a mural on the sides and top and a face on the hood. "We'd go to the drive-in movies. I could get 10 friends in the car and four in the trunk." After high school, Foust spent his college days majoring in advertising and tooling around in a 41,000-mile, one-owner '55 Coupe de Ville. "Everything worked, even the clock and washers," he added. "I drove it through college" and restored three other old Caddys and sold them,

becoming very familiar with the needs of Cadillac restorers.

After college, Foust worked for a couple years on the lube rack at Lone Star Cadillac, a dealership in Dallas, bought the acreage that became his current business address, and as Foust put it, "flopped around from thing to thing. I owned 12 Cadillacs by that time, then bought out Caddy Land Auto Wrecking, Mineral Wells, Texas" and relocated the inventory to his Justin property where the 12 Caddys were stored. Honest John's Caddy Corner was officially launched in 1984.

Inspiration for the name came from a neon sign Foust remembered seeing as a

child in Fort Worth. The sign depicted "a man in a suit, 'Honest John' with outstretched hands and a slogan which Foust remembers as going something like this: "Fair Deal – Square Deal." Drawing on more recent memories from advertising classes in college, Foust knew that a venture into the old car business, especially one involving mail order sales, would benefit greatly from a catchy name such as the one he remembered from childhood. The name Honest John's Caddy Corner was coined and the unusual Caddy-only business venture set sail into a marketing stream that has gained international prestige. ∎

5. Lupe Nava, the paint and body man at Honest John's, preps a pink 1959 Cadillac for a customer who sells for Mary Kay Cosmetics. (Randoll Reagan photo)

6. Anything non-Cadillac is as scarce as chicken's teeth at Honest John's Caddy Corner. This '41 series 63 Sedan is one of the older pieces on hand. Honest John's services a large number of drivers who use later model Cadillacs for daily transportation.

7. A 1947 Cadillac sits next to the '41 pictured at left. Both have bone dry bodies and sheet metal.

8. The fins on this '57 Coupe de Ville were styled with an emphasis on conservatism. The rear fenders slope forward toward the cabin. The elegant '57 is a favorite among Caddy collectors.

9. With pillarless hardtop styling, the 1956 Cadillac Sedan de Ville is a thing of beauty. The year 1956 marked the third and last year for the "C" bodied model introduced in 1954. Sales reached 150,000 in '56; it was a record year at Cadillac.

10. Most U.S. automakers adopted quad headlamps on all production models in 1958. Cadillac was no exception. The paint on this '58 coupe is pretty thin, but the sheet metal is still fresh and tidy.

11. The graceful and sedate lines of the 1941 Cadillac Fleetwood Sixty Special are seen on this old gal whose been put out to pasture at Honest John's Caddy Corner.

12. A '59 flat-top has parted with a few of her parts, but there's a passel left on this finned beauty.

13

13. The Fisher body on this 1964 Sedan de Ville four-window features reserved styling with lots of emphasis on comfort. Traditionally, Caddys have been bought and driven by folks with an above average income and a true appreciation of quality workmanship.

14. A fellow from Mexico City drove up to Honest John's to remove parts from this '53 Cadillac Fleetwood limo. The motor is still there as well as a ton of good parts he elected not to buy.

15. Hailing from the Meteor plant, Piqua, Ohio, this 1950 ambulance featuring a raised roof and custom body was built on a Series 8680S commercial chassis. No trim or paint numbers appear on the body tag. Major body components came from Fisher Body.

14

15

16

16. This 1967 Fleetwood Eldorado represents the first year for front wheel drive from Cadillac. It was a first at Cadillac, but not for a GM car. The 1966 Oldsmobile Toronado holds that distinction.

17. Freshening up old Caddys makes them easier to sell. Most folks don't have body shop facilities and elect to have Honest John and his crew do the work. This '61 sedan will be repainted from stem to stern. In case you're interested, the gal with the quick arm is the author's wife.

18. As the 1960s marched on, fender ridges got more creases along leading edges, reflecting a conscious design theme from GM. This is a '66 Coupe de Villle.

19. Need a nice dry rust-free trunk lid? Honest John's has a number of them as well as a field of other rust-free parts already removed from their host cars.

20. The small round badge on the rear quarter of this Caddy Eldo marks it as a 1968 or newer model. The '67 didn't have the badge. This is a '69.

21

21. Honest John's personal driver is a black mile-long limo. The black beauty stretches "seven paces long," according to Honest John. That's almost 20 feet in length which is too long for many garages.

22. Honest John and his wife Donna cruise to Caddy functions in their limo. They drove the Series 75 limo to New York to a Caddy club meet several years ago and it was a pleasure to drive, he says. It has dual air conditioning units. The factory retail price for the long drink of water was a stout $10,521 in 1966.

22

23

23. Subdued and bossy '74 Cadillac Fleetwood Brougham Talisman has run the course but stiil has horses to spare. There are some pretty nice parts as well. Honest John would prefer to sell this car complete.

24

24. The late Bill Mitchell, former VP of styling at GM, was "accused of stealing the trunk line" from Rolls for the Elegante Seville of the early '80s. His retort was quick and sharp – "My dad always told me – If you're going to rob someone, don't rob a liquor store, rob a bank." The one pictured here is an '81.

25. Most convertibles are stored in rows in front of the shop.

26. Overall the ragtops are pretty solid and complete, save for a few parts that John pulled to satisfy customers.

27. Supplying cars and parts for daily drivers has become a good source of income for Honest John's Caddy Corner. In the '70s row, '72, '76 and '78 Coupe de Villes wait for parts buyers. In many parts of the country driving "big O" Cadillacs has become trendy. Honest John swears by their dependability.

28.

28. John says the glass in this 1966 Cadillac Crown Sovereign is "worth a fortune in resale." The curved corners are pricey at $225 each and up. The rear sides go for around $150 each.

29. She's been here for quite a while – just sits around, starving for attention, but she doesn't eat much anymore. Venerable '47 is very patient and willing to wait for any affection she can garner.

30. Honest John took the author to lunch at the Ranchman's cafe, a local legendary eatery in Ponder, Texas. The actors and film crew for the movie *Bonnie and Clyde* dined and worked near the Ranchman's during the filming of the blockbuster. The late "Pete" Jackson entertained many celebrities over the years, i.e. former U.S. President Jimmy Carter and his wife and other famous and monied personalities. Honest John's daily driver is a metallic green 1967 Coupe de Ville in gorgeous condition. And for those of you who do not believe that lightning strikes twice in the same location... as we dined, another film crew approached Honest John to use his '67 in the movie *Take It Like a Man* which will be released in the fall of 1999.

29.

30.

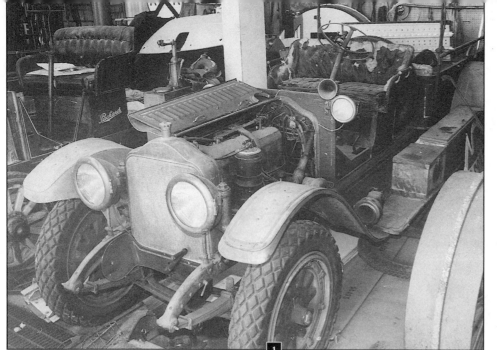

Photos by the author

1. This aging '15 White fire truck is still on Ersland's not-for-sale list. "I would buy more like it, if I could find them," he says. There were only 300 or so built. This piece was used to fight fires in Brainerd, Minn.

## A mailman who dragged home a few finds over the years

# Joe Ersland Antique Cars

## Chickasha, Oklahoma

2. The youthful Joe Ersland poses beside a WW II vintage White half-track that may have served at Ft. Sill, a nearby military post.

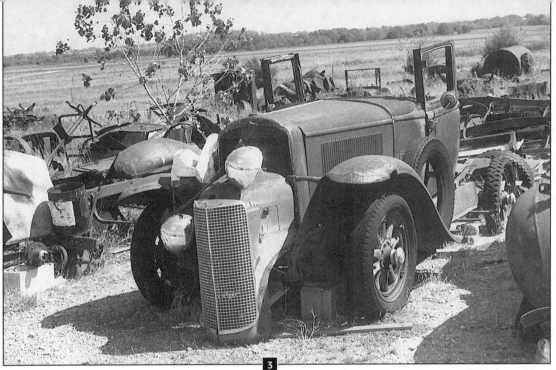

3. The engine in what remains of a 1930 Buick ran the last time Ersland tried it. The pot metal grille standing in front is from a '38 Cadillac.

4. A Case steam tractor sits beside a body for a 1912 White Gas car, built by the White Motor Car Co, Cleveland, Ohio. The Case is not for sale, but the hundreds of signs that have found a home at Ersland's are.

by Ken New

Soft-spoken Joe Ersland has placed around 1,500 cars into the hands of collectors in his 40 years of tinkering with old cars. Ersland's passion for all kinds of older vehicles is pronounced, but the nameplate most dear to his heart is White. Ersland's interest in White began in 1958 when he traded a Ford Model T speedster and $100 for a White Steam car in Carnegie, Okla.

The White is a little known make of car that was built only a few years in the early part of the century by what later became the White Motor Car Co, Cleveland, Ohio. The early Whites were light, buggy-like vehicles with chain-drive and tiller steering. Most were steampowered, but a few built later were gas-powered. All Whites were outstanding cars in their day, but automobile production took a back seat to truck production at White and the last White car was built in 1910 as a 1911 model. Truck production lasted into the 1990s.

Trading old cars and parts has provided a means for Ersland to fuel his White collecting habits. To date, he has owned 34 Whites; a fair amount considering a registry maintained by the Horseless Carriage Club of America lists only 140 in existence.

Ersland's collection is stored at two locations in Chickasha, Okla., a community located in southwestern Oklahoma where dry conditions exist most of the year. Severe rust is a rarity. The collection consists of a number of interesting

## ABOUT THE YARD

Joe Ersland Antique Cars, P.O. Box 562, Chickasha, OK 73023-0562, phone 405-224-2049, 405-222-3047 or 405-779-7108, is owned and operated by Joe and Sandy Ersland. Ersland's inventory reflects his interest in very old cars and trucks. Other automotive collectibles, oil signs, etc., are available as well. Chickasha, Oklahoma is located north of Wichita Falls, Texas and southeast of Oklahoma City, Oklahoma on I-44. For specific directions and to make an apppointment, call ahead. Note: Chickasha is pronounced Chick-a-shay. Ersland prefers not to ship cars or parts.

cars, a fair amount of auto memorabilia and an unusual and spectacular assortment of heavy old trucks not commonly seen in most collections. Many of the trucks date back into the early teens while others range to the '50s. It's rare to find an older truck that is in pristine condition since most examples remaining were worked hard and have scars to prove it. They usually need a lot of restoration but, oftentimes, in the eyes of rabid truck collectors, rarity makes the tolls and trials of restoration worthwhile, at least in a personal satisfaction mode rather than a financial one. Typically, trucks don't attract the attention or the big bucks that cars do.

Ersland is first and foremost a collector and has never dealt in cars as a means of support. For many years he was a rural mail carrier covering a daily 90-mile route that took him to many remote areas of Oklahoma where he found and gathered up old cars and parts. Many of the old cars and parts were given to him just to get them out of sight. Many were bought for $25 to $45.

Since Ersland's retirement from the U.S. Postal Service in 1980, he has devoted more time to his hobby. An '09 White Model M, purported to be the oldest and largest steam-powered car of its model in existence, has been a joy of his retirement. Its restoration has been very difficult due to a lack of parts and Ersland's determination to restore it correctly. More than 15 years have been spent on its ongoing restoration, which Ersland hopes to finish soon.

Ersland believes his part of the country and "on north into Canada" is a good place to buy old cars and parts. They aren't too rusty and the sellers are very friendly people. Currently, Ersland has "about a hundred vehicles; 90 percent are stored outside. And, I have 10-15 that I won't sell," he says. Most of the latter have a White nameplate on them. ■

5. The remnants of an extremely rare 1901 Searchmont, a car built in Philadelphia, Pa. (1900-1903), is in the Ersland collection. This vehicle may have been the one entered in the AAA Endurance Run in 1901, although that has not been documented. The Searchmont failed to complete the historic test. Of the 81 cars entered, only 41 finished the run. Four White Steam cars were declared winners with each awarded a first-place certificate.

6. Looking for potential? This 1939 Cadillac coupe may be the answer. The bumpers are not for this car. They are for a 1940 Caddy.

7. Big old '41 Caddy is from the Series 63 line. This is a rather rare car as only this body style was offered in the Series 63 line in 1941. It is very restorable.

8. Rare Smith Oil pump was used up into the '60s. A hint of a "We Give Green Stamps" decal is posted on one side. The pump sits next to a 1915 Packard.

9-10. There are approximately 10 gas pumps and a large number of oil cans and related items stored here.

**11.** The red and yellow porcelain Shell sign hasn't lost its brightness after all these years. It dates to the 1930s. Tire or tire covers dating to 1907 hang from nails below.

**12.** Ersland's collection of oil-related memorabilia is extensive. Seen here are five-gallon cans, a couple of gas pumps and a good assortment of large grease cans, plus a few signs.

**13.** Need an engine for a Stutz 8? Ersland has a pair of them, one for a 1931 and one for a '28.

**14.** This Ford sign hails from the early '20s. The scratches and bruises add to its charm.

15. Once a working fire truck, this 1913 White would be magnificent in fire engine red all dolled up with gold leaf and polished brass.

16. Ersland's dream to restore his 1932 Cadillac V-16 Town Car was laid aside when he found out how expensive it would be to finish it properly.

17. A fondness for old beasts of burden is obvious at Ersland's collection. He has owned this 1915 Packard truck for 12 years.

18. This chassis from the early '30s is for a Cadillac V-16. It was bought years ago at the famed Hershey Fall swap meet. It doesn't have an engine.

19. Cars don't suffer much from rust around this part of Oklahoma, even in outside storage. This red '71 Ford convertible has been whacked along the front fender, but the rust-free fender is worth fixing.

20. Most trim parts used on 1951 and '52 Chevrolets are interchangeable. This '51 slope back has a '52 grille in it.

21. Ersland says this White truck dates to the early '20s and is probably a two or three tonner.

**22.** The awkward no-nonsense box on this 1934 Dodge Railway Express truck seems to add to the pretence that it lumbers along even at rest. The front fenders have been clipped.

**23.** This '49 White C.O.E. has a dump bed and lots of macho charisma. A heavyweight GMC from the early '50s sits to the rear.

**24.** In its day, the 1953 Plymouth Cambridge, although stodgy, was considered a very dependable piece of transportation.

**25.** Another piece of dependable transportation was the 1954 Chevy, but it is much more handsome, even as a four-door model, than the Plymouth.

**26.** Wouldn't this old Diamond T be a great restoration project? It's of either '36 or '37 vintage, according to Ersland, who says placing exact year dates on trucks is very difficult since truck manufacturers rarely got tied up in new model hype.

**27.** This 1942 Ford C.O.E. from Enid, Oklahoma was driven to Ersland's place a few years ago. It has its original engine.

**28.** This low mile '35 Mack was used as a fire truck in Minco, Oklahoma before it took the 18 mile drive to Chickasha and Ersland's.

**29.** The remains of a GMC from about '24 or '25 are probably of a 3/4-ton type, according to Ersland. The letters GMC are cast into the engine.

26

27

28

29

30. For more than 40 years, Ersland has collected White vehicles. This 1930 White truck was bought in Indiana for $500.

31. Aluminum was used to shroud the radiator of this 1929-31 White. Some of the engine parts are missing. The '37 Diamond T in the background has a 472 Cadillac engine under the hood.

32. An F20 Gold Comet Reo truck is fairly straight, having never been subjected to close work where it would have been abused by scrapes and dents.

33. Tough and tall late '40s White Mustang was last plated in 1978, having labored for many years before being retired. The IH wrecker in the background is WW II vintage.

34. Any vehicle driven by steam is welcomed at Ersland's. This group of farm tractors, etc., wears names like Port Huron, Adams Scaper, and Indiana.

35. Have you ever heard of a Moreland? Not many prople have. This stark beast is a 1928 Moreland.

36. Here is a pride and joy of Joe Ersland and his son Mike, an '09 White Model M. It is the oldest, largest steam car in the world and is not for sale at any price. The old White came from the famed Fred Buess collection in 1970. The ongoing restoration started in the mid-'80s.

37. Ersland has a 1929 Ford AA with an assortment of household items aboard that makes it look like it could have been used in the Grapes of Wrath movie. During the '30s, drought reduced the Okie state to a dust bowl and lots of folks moved on to California.

38. If it's the unusual you seek, here's one of the rarest vehicles around. It's a 1928 Willys-Knight with a sleeve-valve motor.

39. Here's another strange one, an Eclipse built by the Frick Co. of Waynesboro, Pa.

36

37

38

39

Photos by the author

1. Bill Johnson (left), owner of Johnson's Wrecker & Salvage, poses alongside his 1937 Lincoln Zephyr coupe, with long-time friend Joe Ersland. The coupe was purchased more than 20 years ago in Grand Junction, Colo. In near original condition, the Zephyr still has original paint on the under side of the hood.

## A source for dry rust-free cars that has rarely been tapped

# Johnson's Wrecker Service

## Chickasha, Oklahoma

2. A 1950 Cadillac Coupe de Ville is a handsome car from any angle. Only 10,241 were built in 1950. Other cars in this photo are a Pontiac Bonneville convertible, another early Caddy, a commercial bodied rig and a couple of late '40s Mercs.

by Ken New

Bill Johnson has a soft spot for Lincoln V-12s. He has owned more than 25, "maybe 30", over the years and still owns a few. Presssed as to how many of the venerable flatheads he now owns, Johnson is slow to answer. "Well, " he begins, then stops, seemingly hesitant to speak in specific numbers, "about six or eight," he says, shifting into a slightly higher gear. The inexact nature of his answers never seems to bother this 71-year-old Oklahoman whose interest in the V-12 was honed when he began working in his father's repair garage when he was 16. Those six or eight V-12s include '41 and '47 Lincoln Continental convertibles, a '47 coupe and the magnificent, almost original 1937 V-12 pictured in this story. "I've bought and sold V-12s all my life it seems, but I don't have a favorite car. I like "em all," he volunteers and then stops abruptly, saying no more about the other V-12s.

Bill Johnson is a busy man with several business interests that have made it impossible for him to retire, "even though I've thought about it," he says referring to the seven-day-a-week wrecker service which keeps him hopping in and out of his cinder block building location in Chickasha, Okla.

Johnson's wrecker service and salvage business is located within a short distance of I-44, a pipeline of commerce that flows north into Oklahoma City. In between wrecker service calls, Johnson and his crew of three interact with walk-in traffic responding to the hoard of old cars they have spotted sitting alongside South Hwy. 81 within Chickasha's city limits.

If you wish to contact Johnson about an old car, be advised that he runs the salvage business as a sideline to his wrecker service and he doesn't respond favorably to out-of-towners who make appointments, then don't show. The best advice we can give you is to phone ahead and advise Johnson of your interest and impending arrival, then head to Chickasha with adequate time on your hands to idle some away. Once you've arrived, don't be surprised to find Johnson out on a wrecker service run, but be patient and wait on this gentle, yet very busy man. Johnson's old cars, complete or as parts cars, are relatively rust-free and worthy of restoration. Only complete cars are sold, as Johnson doesn't part cars out anymore. "We haven't in many years," adds his son Jimmy, one of the wrecker operators. ■

3. A project waiting for Johnson's attention is a 1940 Mercury convertible. Most of the parts to restore the Merc are stowed inside the car although some shown here are for other cars at Johnson's. A '40 Merc has windwings; a '39 does not.

4. A 1952 Cadillac funeral coach with custom body would be a dandy to restore since it's so solid and straight. Can you imagine a better way to take your last earthly ride than in this elegant tank?

## ABOUT THE YARD

Johnson's Wrecker Service, 3602 So. Hwy. 81, Chickasha, OK 73018, phone 405-224-2800 is owned and operated by Bill Johnson. Chickasha is located on I-44 roughly midway between Wichita Falls, Texas and Oklahoma City, Oklahoma. Towing of heavy to light vehicles is the mainstay of Johnson's business. Salvage is a sideline. Only complete vehicles are sold. Johnson's facilities are located within the Chickasha city limits on Hwy. 81 South. Business hours are Monday-Friday 9:30 a.m. to 5:30 p.m. Johnson doesn't make special appointments. Delivery of vehicles is available. Note: Chickasha is pronounced Chick-a-shay.

5. Close up of the Merc from photo 2 shows a four-door sedan with some restoration completed and a lot to go before she's done. One of Johnson's wreckers can be seen at the top of the photo.

6. Another dry Caddy sits nearby. This one is a '53 with the distinctive dagmars up front.

7. A four-door Merc from the late '40s sits near the front of the wrecker station. Johnson has five Mercs of this vintage. All are restorable with great potential.

8. Old Buick from either '47 or '48 is not one of the most desirable body styles, but its condition is right at the top.

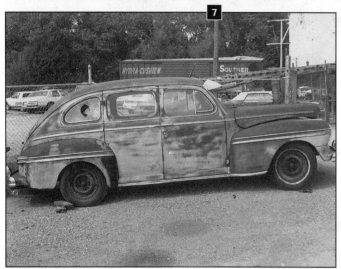

9. Johnson's passion for old Mercs and Lincolns has caused him to hook onto many and drag them home. There are two 1940 Mercury sedans at Johnson's.

10. The engine in this 1947-48 Lincoln has been removed and the hood stacked on top of the car, but it still has an appealing look to collectors.

11. A '58 Ford Skyliner flip-top convertible shows more sun damage than anything else. The body is mostly rust-free and pretty straight. The top mechanism is very complete, and these systems rarely need much to restore them to working order.

12. Green and white '55 Olds 88 four-door is another family sedan from GM, but trimmed out a bit classier.

13. Chevy's unglamorous plain jane family sedan for 1957 was the 210 four door.

14. Glancing at those letters on the trunk lid, Mustangers will say this one is a '67, but it's not. It's a '68 with a '67 lid. The '68 didn't have the individual letters.

15. A cute '62 Falcon Ranchero sits out by the fence along Highway 81, which runs north and south through Chickasha.

16. This '54 Buick has some of the nicest bumpers and front brightwork we've seen in a long time considering there's a zillion pieces that could have gotten damaged over the years. The chrome is lacking luster, but so what?

17. Blue '39 Mercury two-door has the wide-five wheels Ford used from '36 thru '39 and no wind wings. The bumper guard is aftermarket. The solid old Merc wears a '68 Oklahoma plate.

18. If only this '53 were a Skylark, they'd be beating down the doors at Johnson's. It's one of the most restorable cars we've seen.

19. This old soldier from Ford was built during World War II sometime between 1942 and 1945 when styling changes were discontinued. It sits in a grove of mini sunflowers.

20. If you're into old cars, there's gotta be something in this photo that excites you. Most of the cars are of GM manufacture with a Rambler in the mix. If you don't find a car to love, you've at least got to like their rust-free condition.

21. A doorless '55 Chevy Bel Air hardtop has a number of desirable parts left for salvaging.

22. Out back of the garage, Johnson is adding fill dirt and closing in on a foursome consisting of three Chevy cars and a Chevy pickup.

23. Grounded but not pounded, this '55 DeSoto Fireflite sedan has sheet metal rust belt dwellers would die for.

24. The pristine tin on this Pontiac hardtop from 1951 is practically ready for stripping down for paint.

Photos by the author unless noted otherwise

1. A 1957 Ford Fairlane four-door sedan at Country Auto has some pretty nice sheet metal and small parts. This one could be made to go.

## Melba Holik defies the gender gap and runs a salvage operation

# Country Auto

## Chandler, Oklahoma

by Ken New

2. Melba Holik of Country Auto, Chandler, Okla. keeps up a long family tradition of working in the automobile business. Holik's father Kenneth and his brothers sold their Studebaker dealership in the late '50s and bought a garage, service station and salvage business. The small plaque Holik holds is from the old Studebaker dealership. Holik grew up in her father's shadow and knows cars inside and out.

Country Auto, a salvage operation in Chandler, Okla., shows few signs of the Studebaker dealership that baptized a Sooner family into the automobile business in the early 1950s. Owner Melba (Sherman) Holik is the current caretaker of a salvage business started by Holik's father and his four brothers back in the late '50s when hard times visited the Studebaker empire and shook the automaker to its knees, laying waste to Studebaker dealerships by the hundreds – including the Shermans' in Chandler.

With no means to save their Studebaker business, the Shermans decided to sell the dealership and purchase a salvage, service station and garage business. It was a good decision. The brothers assumed various responsibilities with Melba's father Kenneth taking over the garage division. By the early '70s, when Melba joined the business, the salvage operation was maintained only as part of the repair division and it wasn't profitable on its own. Holik begin to explore used car sales as a means to make the business more profitable and about the same time, she was involved in an accident with her six-year-old Dodge Dart. When she began to search salvage yards in the area for parts to fix her Dart, she was surprised to find no spares available. Inventories contained older cars with few newer wrecks in stock. Holik says her accident and search for parts was a turning point. "I got out of used cars and begin to buy every old Dart I could find," planning to never be in that helpless situation again. She never was caught short again; even made money selling the

## ABOUT THE YARD

Country Auto, Rt. 4, Box 125A, Chandler, OK 74834, phone 405-258-0957 or 405-567-3105 is owned and operated by Melba Holik. Holik's yard is located south of Chandler. From I-44, hit Hwy. 18 at exit 166 and drive south 4-1/2 miles to Country Auto. It's on the right. Business hours vary by appointment. Call ahead. Holik prefers to sell complete cars although some cars are available for parting out. Parts are removed by one of Holik's associates or by special arrangement with the buyer.

3. A '53 Packard Clipper sedan is complete except for a few items. Lower body panels are fairly solid. Some surface rust is showing in this photo.

4. A white front fender replaced sometime in the past but never painted prompts one to question the original color of this '62 Chevy hardtop. It was black. Replacing a smashed driver's door would do wonders for this baby.

4. A local farmer near Country Auto quit driving his KB2 International pickup when the brakes failed. A few minor fixes and she'd be issued a new work card.

6. There was a drizzle of rain the day we visited Country Auto. The glare dancing on the hood of this '53 Studebaker two-door post sedan highlights the slight surface rust on this basically solid car.

7. This is about as nice a '57 Ford Custom Cab F100 as we've seen in a salvage yard. The paint is fading, but the pickup appears to be complete and restorable. It has a rebuilt motor.

spares, she says. Then, feeling pretty good about her success, she began to stock up on all kinds of older cars "especially '68 Galaxies to keep her husband's car on the road," and to supply parts to the growing collector car market. Meantime, Holik was laying back some of her favorite cars and buying the parts she'd need to restore them sometime in the future.

Recently, Holik introduced Country Auto to a new marketing strategy – selling vintage cars and parts on the internet. She believes her webpage can bring customers from far-away places, buyers who may have never considered Chandler, Okla. as a place where old cars and parts can be purchased. Now with her new priorities, Holik figures she'll never find time to restore all her cars and is willing to part with some of them. "The one thing people like about my cars is they are basically complete." Country Auto's new web page address is www.expage.com/page/countryauto. Should you contact Country Auto via the internet, Holik would appreciate an inquiry that is very specific. You should provide as much detail as necessary and indicate the price range you are expecting to pay. It'll save time for both you and Holik. On the other hand, if you contact Country Auto through normal channels, expect to talk with a lady who knows collector cars very well and is known for fair dealings. ∎

8. There's still life under that flesh pink and white skin of this 1958 Packard, a coupling of Studebaker and Packard components resulting from the two automakers combining forces.

9. Here's a one-owner Ford AA truck. It has more or less settled in here at Country Auto, having been here for more than 20 years.

10

10. A '53 Chevy Bel Air hardtop shows a hint of that luscious goldenrod yellow paint Chevrolet offered in '53.

11. This '50 Ford two-door at Holik's yard has been hot rodded a bit in its life, but it's rarin' to go again.

12. This tired old '54 Ford F100 was well optioned out from the factory. It had Ford's "new in '54" ohv V-8, a radio and spare wheel carrier.

13. A few trim items and small parts are about all that's left to salvage on this black and white 1956 Ford Victoria four-door hardtop.

11

12

13

14. Cowboys like pickups, right? One trimmed and whacked this '58 Thunderbird into a Ranchero quite some time ago. The old 'Bird is a bit landlocked, don't you think? The cottonwood is post Vietnam era.

15. There are five 1953 Buicks at Country Auto. Reportedly this hardtop is a 32,000 low miler. A doghouse to finish out the front end is available.

16. A few parts are scattered about the yard. Here's a grille for a '54 Chevy pickup and one for a '52 Pontiac. Both are very desirable.

17. Lovable old Studebaker from the early '50s needs a bunch of hammer and dolly work on its reasonably solid body and a nice finish to make it look new again.

18. Taking a bow into the grass is this '57 Triumph roadster that hails from Missouri. Country Auto has several European car makes represented in its collection of cars. A replacement for the Triumph's damaged front sheet metal sits on the hood of the Buick to the left.

19. Power aboard this '67 Plymouth Belvedere is the big block 383. There's a lot of potential in this one.

20. Well punched and put out to pasture, this '66 Chevy Series 10 has seen better days. It has a number of salvageable parts left.

21. The owners of Country Auto purchase parts to complete their cars whenever possible. The headlamps on this 1937 Pontiac sedan came from the Chickasha Swap Meet, Chickasha, Okla.

22. Classy '58 Mercedes-Benz sedan wears a frowning front bumper. It needs someone to love and care for it.

23. Country Auto has five Flip-Top Fords including this desirable '57. A package deal can be made for all five of them. (Melba Holik photo)

24. Regal black '55 Studebaker President bears a '64 California plate but no motor. Sadly, the fellow who extracted the engine chopped the grille to make the job easier.

25. The rear fender damage found on this '67 Dodge Coronet 500 occurred after it came to Country Auto. Otherwise, it could use some exterior trim and tlc. It has a 318 aboard.

26. A very particular Mopar collector drove to Country Auto to check the numbers on this 1973 Plymouth Satellite Sebring hardtop with vinyl roof. He wanted a particular combination, which the Texas car didn't have.

1

# Charlie Reinert's Garage

## Pottstown, Pennsylvania

By Eric Brockman

Charlie Reinert's little service station in Pottstown, Pa. sits in stark contrast to the "super mart" service stations of the '90s. This piece of a forgotten age represents a dying breed — the independent corner service station. Everything looks much as it must have during America's "golden age" following World War II, right down to the vintage Chevy wrecker.

Looking at the photos here, you might have guessed that Charlie likes Corvairs. In fact, it's been his specialty pretty much since Chevy's unique little rear-engined compact debuted in the fall of 1959. But after more than five decades in opera-

2

**Photos by the author**

1-2. Is it 1999 or 1959? Charlie Reinert's service station still looks much as it might have in the '50s. Reinert bought the Chevy wrecker new! Like many similar service stations, this one may soon be disappearing from the landscape.

3. Reinert loves Corvairs, as this shot of the garage's surrounding lot attests. Since our visit, most of these cars were sold at auction. A handful of Corvairs (cars and vans) remains.

4. Corvairs came in many shapes and sizes, including vans. Reinert had a row of these forgotten Corvairs at his garage. He said he still has nine vans, all of which are for sale.

## ABOUT THE YARD

Charlie Reinert's Garage is an old landmark at the corner of Farmington Avenue and East Street in Pottstown, Pa., a town of some 23,000 right off I-422 about 25 miles northwest of Philadelphia. The phone number is 610-326-1084.

tion, Reinert decided its time to hang up his wrenches. In fact, most — if not all — of the vehicles depicted here have already been sold or parted out. But some cars do remain, and he has a large assortment of parts.

We visited Reinert's garage-cum-Corvair salvage yard in October of 1996; the following June, he held a two-day auction, selling many cars and parts. He has slowly been selling what remains ever since then. When we recently spoke to him on the phone, he reported that he has four cars, nine vans, and several trailer-loads of parts. While most parts are for Corvairs, he does have parts for other makes and models as well.

He said he's willing to sell the remainder of his inventory piece-by-piece if necessary, but he would also entertain offers on the whole lot. He also plans to sell the garage itself, which sits on 3/4 of an acre in Pottstown. Perhaps someone will step forward, and keep a portion of American automobile history alive.

Anyone interested in talking to Charlie Reinert about inventory and prices can contact him at 610-326-1084. ∎

5. Rows of air-cooled, rear-engined Chevy compacts fill the lot at Reinert's Garage. Most of these cars have been sold, but several good examples remain.

6. Reinert had a number of unusual pieces, including this station wagon. When was the last time you saw one of these on the highway?

7. One of the more desirable pieces in Reinert's collection was this turbocharged Spyder. It had a lot of rust and was missing some parts.

8-9. Corvairs aren't Reinert's only love — he also has an affinity for vintage Cadillacs. His personal collection includes this '49 sedan and a beautiful '37 V-8 sedan.

Photos by the author

1. Yard owner Joe Downey poses alongside a 1949 Olds 76 two-door sedan. It's restorable but it's not for sale. Joe wants to restore this one himself ... it was his first car, not one like, but the actual car he bought in 1962 at the age of 16. He blew the engine years ago, and parked it. But he has since acquired a correct replacement engine.

## Western Ohio yard offers a wide variety

# Graveyard II Auto Parts and Sales

## Coldwater, Ohio

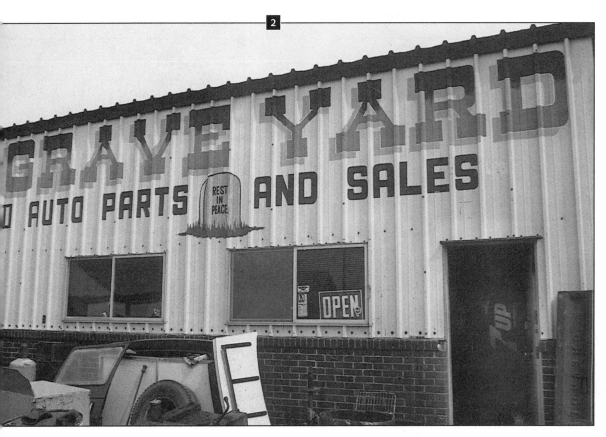

2. Graveyard Auto Parts is a resting place — the final resting place in most cases — for tired old cars and trucks. The yard, in Coldwater, Ohio, is filled with vintage iron.

by Bob Stevens

Nestled onto a 35-acre site in west central Ohio, Graveyard II Auto Parts reflects, to a great extent, the varied interests of its owner, Joe Downey, who has a strong preference for Packards, Hudsons, Studebakers, Buicks and Oldsmobiles. And there are many examples of all those makes from the '50s and '60s, and even back into the '40s and '30s.

The yard itself is quartered on a 14-acre tract, leaving lots of room for a buffer zone and for future expansion. And, Joe Downey is always scouting out new iron in the yards that he crushes. One of his primary business pursuits is the crushing of salvage yards throughout Ohio, using a fleet of portable crushers. When he moves into a yard, he ferrets out any decent old iron and hauls it away, with the owner's consent of course, and puts it into his yard for either resale or use as a parts car. It's an efficient way to build inventory.

Just recently the yard added a huge collection of old Packards, 25 in all, ranging from the late '40s up to 1956, the last of the real Packards. There are several two-door hardtops in the mix. Downey, who has owned several show-quality Packards, has a real soft spot for the celebrated marque. He found the cache of Packards buried in a back corner of a yard of late model cars he crushed in northeast Ohio. He transported the 25

3. Lane leading from the shop back to the yard is fenced on one side, and the fence is decorated with wheel covers and hubcaps of all types and years.

## ABOUT THE YARD

Graveyard II Auto Parts, 3383 Kuhn Rd., Coldwater, Ohio 45828, is owned and operated by Joseph R. Downey. The yard is open normal business hours. Call 419-586-1367. From the north, take I-75 south to 33 west. Stay on 33 west as it turns into 29 and goes into Celina, where you'll pick up 127 and head south. At 219, turn right and head west to 118 in Coldwater, where you turn right and go north to the third crossroad, which is Kuhn Road. Turn left and go about three miles; Graveyard is on the right or north side of the road. From the south, take I-75 north to 219 (Botkins exit) and head west, follow 219 signs to four-way stop, turn right and go north to 219, turn left, head west to Coldwater. In Coldwater, turn right at the Catholic Church onto 118 and head north to Kuhn Road.

4. For the most part, cars are neatly arranged in rows. There is some thick underbrush to deal with, but every car is accessible.

5. Graveyard II's owner, Joe Downey has kept a Franklin sedan under cover for many years. He'd loved to see the girl restored. This shot of the unusual air-cooled engine speaks for the general condition of the car.

6. A "Be Sure with Pure" sign is holding up a small outbuilding, or vice versa.

7. A '62 Ford convertible hopes for better days ahead. There is a lot of useful stuff still on this car, including a top frame.

8. Pontiac LeMans coupes huddle together in a remote section of the yard. The operation's owner has tried to keep cars of the same make and model grouped together to simplify and expedite the search for parts.

Packards some 200 miles to get them to his yard.

There are more than 1,900 cars in the Graveyard operation, which has been in business since 1972. A few of the cars are restorable, but most are primarily useful for parts. Some are newer, with a lot of '70s cars, but more than 400 are 1964 or older, and a few out of the '30s can be spotted in the yard. Walking through this yard is like taking a trip back in time, to about the mid-'60s when today's antiques were the late model wrecks of the day. It's like a supermarket for old car parts ... just be sure to bring a very large and sturdy shopping cart. ■

9

9. Some cars have already been beheaded! Most, though, are still wearing their original tops.

10. Fairly solid and complete '63 Chevy two-door sedan is fighting to fend off Mother Nature's embracing arms. Interior was pretty much all there, including a complete dash.

11. It's a ragtop, and its top is really in rags. This '63 Ford convertible has only a fair body, but there's lots of other good stuff present and accounted for, and waiting for the taking.

12. Some of the caps hooked to the fence are of the more appealing variety, such as the Buick wire caps seen here (upper right).

10

11

12

13. The yard is located in a remote section of the county, surrounded by cornfields and other agricultural properties.

14. A 1938 Packard front clip hopes to someday be reunited with a Packard of the same year and style.

15. A '64 Pontiac Catalina has barely been tapped for parts, while the '59 Pontiac Star Chief four-door sedan in the background has already yielded a few major items.

16. A Pontiac Firebird sport coupe, circa late '70s, almost looks as though it could be driven away with a new set of tires, a fully-charged battery and some fresh gas.

17. The yard is spread over 14 acres, but it's on a 35-acre site so there's room for future expansion if the business and the inventory require it.

18. Most of this 1951 Hudson Hornet is still hanging on the car, but it's in pretty sad shape.

19. Red and white '57 Studebaker is a President four-door sedan, and it's pretty much all there.

20. With its top erect in an informal salute, this Buick convertible awaits parts hunters.

Photos by the author

1. Gene Shore's typical day is a real whirlwind of activity, i.e. taking care of customers in need of mechanical repair, such as alternators, brake jobs, etc., pumping gas, selling sodas, taking phone calls and selling vintage car parts from the salvage yard located across the road.

# An old time salvage yard that's run as a sideline

# H. Shore & Sons Garage

## Modoc, Indiana

by Ken New

Gene Shore was busy closing in on an electrical problem plaguing a farm truck when we arrived at Shore's general repair garage and salvage facility. The block building from which Gene and his brother Russell conduct business has a "meant for business" air about it. Nothing fancy here to distract from the business at hand – repairing sick vehicles and selling old car parts. On the left side of the shop, service bays are located. A filling station takes up the right corner.

Bill and Paul Hughes, Muncie, Ind., my hosts for the day, recalled visits to Shore's back in the '60s and had offered to bird dog the place prior to our visit to the rural Indiana yard. The office is just like it was back in the '50s and in itself is worth a visit even if you aren't out to buy parts. There's a pair of dark green vinyl and chrome chairs with a convenient smoking stand sitting squared up to a graying oak desk. Through the plate glass window, gas customers can be seen easily. An aging soda machine stocked with soft drinks and a glass showcase full of tasty snacks are right at hand. Ball-point pens, tire gauges, sun glasses and dusty do-dads line the walls. Well-used automotive service manuals are lined up along the book shelves.

In 1933, the late Herman Shore

2. Paul Hughes (left) and Bill Hughes, brothers from Muncie, Ind., got a real kick out of the office, which they say is just like it was 30 years ago when they scrounged the yard for parts to keep their cars running.

started the business in the hamlet of Modoc and moved it out to the main highway in 1954, where it sits today. Over the years, wrecked and tired cars have been pulled in, choice parts pulled to repair others in the shop, then the remains snaked across US 36 to the storage lot. There's some 400-450 cars stored here and Gene doesn't mind if customers stroll through the field of cars in search of parts.

The inventory of cars and trucks is made up predominately of U.S. makes from the '50s with others dating up to the early '70s. A sprinkling of VW Bugs and vans was found. It appears that several cars have been around for quite some time. Sheet metal is pretty rusty, especially on those pieces nearest the ground, while brightwork and trim are generally straight and very salvageable. Most cars aren't picked clean of badges and trim with the exception of the popular Chevy and Ford models, which are pretty well stripped of grilles, taillights, etc. ∎

**3. This Monterey four-door sedan represents the top-of-the-line luxury for Mercury in 1953.**

**4. More mechanically than cosmetically, the 1946 and 1947 Chevrolets were very similar. No side trim and horizontal grille bars identify this beast as a '47 issue.**

## ABOUT THE YARD

H. Shore & Sons Garage, P.O. Box 96, Modoc, IN 47358, phone 765-853-5141, is owned and operated by Gene and Russell Shore, sons of the late Herman Shore, who started the business in 1933. Complete mechanical service is the mainstay of the business. Salvage is a sideline. H. Shore's facilities are located southeast of Muncie, Ind. on Rt. 36 just west of Hwy. 1. Weekday business hours are 6:30 a.m. to 6:30 p.m. (EST). Saturday hours are 7 a.m. to 6 p.m. Closed on Sunday. Customers are allowed to pull parts. Bring your hand tools but leave the fire wrenches at home. Torching parts is handled by one of the Shore brothers.

**5. Seeing a '54 Dodge convertible resting in a yard within a short drive of Indianapolis' famed brickyard where the Dodge paced the Indianapolis 500 Memorial Day race in 1954 causes oldtimers to wonder if this one had any connection with the famed event.**

6. Little of the floor is left in this high riding '56 Chevy two-door post. The sumacs and ground cover have grown up and out of the cavities above.

7. The holes where the horizontal styled parking lamps were mounted denote this car as one of the Plymouth models and not one of the Dodges, which featured squarish lamps. Basic sheet metal with slight differences was shared by the pair.

8. At Shore's, the aisles are mowed regularly for easy access to the parts cars. Yet up close, tall grasses and small brush are left unchecked. Here a 1953 Chevy two-door sedan rests quietly in the weeds.

9. A real runner in its day, this 1952 Hudson Super Wasp hides its nose in the bushes. In 1952, after more than 30 years of use, Hudson dropped the Super Six moniker in favor of Wasp badges.

10. Selected trim and appointments tag this '56 Buick as one built in the Roadmaster line.

11. A few 1970 vintage cars reside at Shore's Garage. This 1973 Mercury Cougar was abandoned, but shows no signs of ever being wrecked. It appears to be in near running condition.

12. A VW Beetle with sun roof from the mid-'60s is gobbled up by an aggressive bank of vines. Gleening would be a bit tough here.

13. A decent pair of patches from the rear quarters and the trunk floor could be taken from this 1955 Chevrolet four-door sedan.

14

14. Ripening blackberries shared this part of the yard with a '55 Cadillac. There's still a bunch of choice items on this old Caddy.

15. Although fitted with a less than very desirable body style, this four-door Bel Air '60 Chevy had a marvelous bunch of brightwork and exterior trim to offer.

16. Lansing-built '65 Olds is somewhat faded but complete. We've seen much worse looking vehicles on the road. Power brake system was intact.

15

16

17

17. "Vee" on the hood of this 1954 DeSoto four-door sedan marks it as the former home of a Firedome V-8 engine. This model attracted 45,095 buyers in '54.

18. Stripped clean, this '57 Ford — once a gleaming Fairlane 500 model — has been picked about as clean as possible; the remaining pieces are very rusty.

18

19. With its original turquoise paint gleaming, this '54 Merc was a real head turner at the local drive-in restaurants back in the '50s. The drivetrain is gone but the front bumper and some sheet metal are worth saving.

19

20

20. Signs of its original rose color is evident on this '55 Chevrolet Bel Air but few pieces of trim remain. Popular models receive the most attention even in retirement.

21. Red and white 1960 Dodge Phoenix two-door hardtop awaits another visitor in need of parts. The engine was long gone when we arrived.

22. All that remains of a '58 Edsel is a hood found sitting in the bed of an early '50s Ford pickup.

23. This '60 Ford Thunderbird is so disarranged, we wondered if it hadn't met with a terrible accident and been dragged to the yard in pieces.

Photos by the author

1. Gary Raef likes to build sleepers, but the bulging hood concealing a potent 302 Ford engine should warn challengers that the originality of this 1961 Austin-Healey 3000 MK III is suspect.

## Only hand-picked relics reside in this vintage collection

# Raef's Auto Body

### Selma, Indiana

2. This pale green 1940 Ford Deluxe two-door sedan is a real creampuff. It's not often you find one that has not gone under the hammer or paint gun since new. That's Gary Raef in the background. It was impossible to keep up with him.

by Ken New

3

Raef's Auto Body wasn't intended to be a salvage yard in the classic sense. It just happened that way over a period of years when vintage cars just seem to follow owner Gary Raef to his home southeast of Muncie, Ind. Raef, an independent auto body shop operator, collects older vehicles with aspirations to restore or modify them. But, finding time to fullfil his plans gets in the way and his generosity to provide homes for the homeless has somehow gotten out of hand. He has some 40 cars and trucks in various states of repair in his collection. And every one is a hand-picked model that has a collector following. At Raef's, you don't have to go tramping around dull slug models. Here, every one is a winner.

Raef's passion for cars is expressed in the genre of makes that populate his collection. His yard is home to bone stock to modified domestic examples as well as rarely seen foreign ones. Sometimes a hot rodder and sometimes a customizer, as well as a fan of pure stock machines, Raef at the tender age of nine or 10 realized that he wanted to be a body man. Then, pause – read this closely – he chopped his first top at age 12 and the die was set. From his rural Indiana shop, the artistry and precision of his body work has made him famous especially with the custom car crowd in the Midwest.

At the time of our visit, he was finishing up the restoration of a 1970 Plymouth Road Runner and plodding full steam ahead into the modification of a '40 Chevy two-door. Luckily, he took time to show us about the yard. ∎

4

## ABOUT THE YARD

Raef's Auto Body, 9701 E. Co. Rd. 600 South, Selma, Ind. 47383, phone 765-774-4311 (FAX 765-774-3511), is owned and operated by Gary Raef. High quality custom auto body work is Raef's main business, but vintage vehicles have a tendency of following Raef home. Only complete cars are sold. Raef's facilities are located southeast of Muncie, Ind. From Muncie drive South on US 35 for 4 miles and turn left onto Co. Rd. 650 South. Continue to 550 East and turn left. Proceed to 600 South and turn right. Go one mile to the intersection of 600 South and 600 East. Raef's Auto Body is on the right hand corner of the intersection. Weekday business hours are 8 a.m. to 5 p.m. (EST). Saturday hours are flexible. Closed on Sunday.

5

3. The pure lines of the 1967 Chevelle two-door hardtop are pure music to the ears of rat motor fans.

4. Old Studebaker from 1953 is stylish, even in pieces. The Raymond Loewy inspired coupe hailed from South Bend, a hundred miles or so north of Raef's business.

5. Stubby '57 Chevy was once a four-door wagon until Raef shortened it into this custom hauler.

6

7

6. The variety of cars in this small yard is quite extensive. Here's a luxurious mid-'50s Jaguar sedan.

7. A very nice 1961 Falcon Ranchero awaits a buyer. The light duty beauty sold for around $1,800 when new.

8. A second '53 Studebaker coupe at Raef's appears to have a better body than the other one shown in this report.

8

9. Orange Crush is the appropriate lettering on the doors of this Dodge deuce and a half. One of Raef's friends brought the truck to his shop for work, then got married. The big rig waits patiently after a change in plans. It has a 350 Chevy under the hood.

10. Even the lowly Falcon hardtops had classy lines in 1963 as evidenced by this example sitting behind Raef's shop.

11. British car fans pinch yourself. This is a 1956 Austin-Healey 100. It has the distinctive lay down windshield and louvered hood. And, yes, it is in storage and cannot be seen from the road.

12. Trent Hutchinson, another friend of Raef's, stopped in the middle of the project on this primered '46 Chevy coupe.

13. 1953 Ford F-600 flat bed belongs to Raef's 29-year-old son, Mark. He has owned the truck since he was 12 years old.

14. Raef has a special attachment to this 1947 Packard. It was born in the same year as Raef.

15. This tag team of midgets is composed of a legitimate Midget and an Austin. Both shared the same body design in the early '70s.

16. Another long overdue project of some 20 years is this '57 Chevy two-door custom. The top posts have been chopped three inches and the roof skin replaced with one from a '58 Chevy Impala. The owner decided to forego the completion of this machine until a sunnier day.

17. Old dualie, a '35 Ford one-tonner wears its original work shoes. It is mostly original except for the turn signals mounted on the top of the fenders.

18. Tired but not worn out '57 Chevy has the makings of a street sleeper.

19. Chopped and channeled '50 Ford F1 is another "what if" that had three inches peeled from its top and six from its body. A 455 Olds, '70 Nova front clip and the rear from the Olds were lying around at the time, so they were incorporated into the "late one night plan."

20. Raef loves to apply subtle modifications to stock-bodied oldies. This particular '39 Chevy sedan is the property of Rick Hooker. The old stovebolt has received a major modification to the trunk area sheet metal that is so subtle you wonder if it's not a rare stocker that GM built. The doors are suicide style.

Photos by the author

1. Bryant's Auto Parts keeps its staff busy chasing both vintage and current automotive parts. Bryant's is conveniently located within a few miles of I-74 but the yard predates the interstate highway, having been started by the Bryant brothers, Wayne and the late Paul "Junior," in 1959.

# Bryant's Auto Parts

## Westville, Illinois

## At Bryant's, you don't have to buy the whole car just to get a taillight rim.

by Ken New

2. Mike Bryant and his father, Wayne Bryant, pose for a rare photo. Wayne and his wife Pat, not shown, are the owners; Mike is the sales manager.

Unlike anything else, the word "crusher" sends shock waves throughout the old car hobby. The reactions from old car fans are predictable and selfish, oftentimes with little regard for the folks who make a living at salvaging auto parts. In recent years we have watched a number of yard operators come face to face with a conflict between their fondness for saving old cars and the reality of doing business in a climate that is often hostile to their very existence. Many of these yard owners have surveyed their holdings, scrapped those vehicles that get about as much respect as Rodney Dangerfield, then restocked their yards with vehicles that generate revenue on a regular basis.

This scenario played itself out a couple years ago at Bryant's Auto Parts, Westville, Ill., when 3,000 slow movers were identified, then crushed. A lot of cars! Yes, but fortunately a significant number of older cars and trucks made the "save" list and there's still a healthy number of them among the 3,700 currently on hand.

The collector stock at Bryant's is lined

3. Dog houses from a late '70s Camaro and a '64 Chevrolet lie behind the shop. Any and all parts are for sale in this yard. No car or truck is sacred and all can be parted out.

4. Mid '60s Ford F-250 pickup with 292 motor aboard appears to have logged many miles as a camper and probably not in Illinois since the body shows only surface rust.

### ABOUT THE YARD

Bryant's Auto Parts, R.R. 1, Westville, IL 61883, phone 217-267-2124 or 1-800-252-5087, is owned by Wayne and Pat Bryant. Mike Bryant is in charge of customer sales. The business was started in 1959 and is located about 6-1/2 miles south of I-74. From I-74 go south on Hwy. 1. Easy to find, Bryant's is located on the south side of town. Business hours are 8 a.m. to 5 p.m. (CST) weekdays. Saturday hours are 8 a.m. to noon.

up horseshoe-like along the north, south and west fences, out of the busy line of traffic where the yard wranglers routinely pull parts from the newer models, which are arranged in rows out in the center of the horseshoe.

Although Bryant's bread and butter are the sales of parts salvaged from newer stock up into the '90s, it aggressively markets vintage and special interest cars and parts to collectors. The yard's sales manager, Mike Bryant, told us that as many as 10-20 packages of vintage car parts are shipped every business day and the number is on the rise.

Bryant's is conveniently located in the Midwest within a few minutes' drive of I-74. For those who plan a visit to Bryant's, there are a couple rules of which you should be aware. Customers are not permitted to pull parts. And, you

5. Mike Bryant pointed out the barn in the background as the place where the salvage operation was started in 1959 by his uncle Paul and his father, Wayne. A cache of NOS parts are stored in the loft. And, yes, they are for sale.

will be accompanied by one of Bryant's employees when shopping the yard. Thus, it's best to phone ahead prior to your visit. In addition, be advised that out where the vintage tin is stored, there's some pretty tall grass and little effort is made to keep the aisles mowed or the ditches drained – Bryant's knows that old car restorers are accustomed to dealing with temporary inconveniences in their pursuit of rare and valuable parts. Go prepared to deal with both. ■

6. Blue and white '57 Ford Skyliner has been in the yard for a long time and it shows. Sales Manager Mike Bryant said any or all of this car is for sale. Prior to production of the retractable top model at Ford, more than 3,000 names were suggested with Skyliner rising to the top from the final list of 126 names.

7. A more rugged looking vehicle has never been built than the military-inspired Willys Jeep. This civilian Willys version at Bryant's looks roadable. Civilian Jeeps had protruding headlamps and military ones had sunken headlamps. Non-original bucket seats are used.

8. A rather plain vanilla late '50s Studebaker Silver Hawk 6 wears a University Ford/Champaign, Ill. used car badge.

9. This 1972 Triumph Spitfire has been whomped soundly on the driver's side. Yet, through all the twisting and jolting, the windshield remained intact. A previous owner disliked the original green color and chose to finish it in bright red. Does anyone know why?

10. If this '49 Caddy had received a little more care, i.e. lube on the hood hinges, the bent hood which eventually resulted might have been prevented. It might stand pretty tall without being hoisted off the ground.

11. A 1957 DeSoto Fireflite Sportsman two-door retains its distinctive forward thrust lines. Arguably the best looking ungussied-up DeSoto in '57, it found 7,217 buyers.

12. Hailing from the Kansas City, Kansas assembly plant, a 1970 Chevelle with vinyl top has lost its 307-cube V-8 engine.

13. Classy 1963 Ford Thunderbird Landau is decked out in silver with a black vinyl top. The 390 block is long departed.

14

14. Another Kansas City star at Bryant's is this '66 Ford Ranchero that came out of the KC plant powered by a 200-cid, six-cylinder engine.

15. The 1957 Oldsmobile 88 shared with Buick its interesting rear window treatment, which lasted only one year and then disappeared.

16. Wearing custom candy apple red paint and spider-webbed with pinstripes, this '69 Mustang was fitted with front fenders from another 'Stang. They are in better condition than the rest of the car.

17. Late '40s Chrysler New Yorker has good brake lamp and lens and bumpers. One taillight casting is broken, but it's virtually complete.

15

16

17

18. If you like the bigger hot rod Dodges, here's one for you. It's a WH23N, which translates into a Coronet two-door hardtop with 383-cid, Hi-Perf. four-barrel V-8 aboard a '71 rambunctious baby.

19. With mostly original paint, this '54 Plymouth Savoy was straight as an arrow. The only cosmetic piece missing was its upper lip chrome.

20. Dodge built a very distinctive and handsome looking truck in 1971, but you don't often see them at vintage car and truck rallys.

21. A scribble on the side glass of this four-door pillarless 1956 Cadillac Sedan de Ville identifies it as a 1951, which is incorrect. It was the first year for this roof design.

22

22. The sometimes hard life of a salvage yard employee! Heavy rain had created mud and runoff knee-deep at the intersections of the aisles. Here, yardman Dale Dukes tries to wrangle the yard's junkyard buggy, a '78 Datsun 280Z, out of the thick mire as yardman Les Johnson, standing, chuckles at his futile efforts. Frustrated, the pair threw in the towel and sought help.

23. Burned to a crisp, this late model Vette had its drivetrain intact but the skin was wasted. In the background, Dale Dukes and his partner, Les Johnson, head back to the shop for the yard's 4020 John Deere farm tractor to extract the sinking 280Z, pictured above, from the mud's stingy grip.

23

Photos by the author

1. Solid '58 Cadillac has lost many key components, but there's still a lot left, including a carful of sheet metal, and all solid western stuff.

# Rust-free iron abounds in this Vegas yard

by Bob Stevens

With new stock arriving frequently from dry desert communities sprinkled throughout the region surrounding Las Vegas, Nev., Murray's Salvage Co. recycles hundreds of cars and trucks every year. And customers come from all over the U.S. as well as overseas to haul home rust-free cars and parts from the dry western desert.

An article on the Murray operation that appeared a couple of years ago in *Cars & Parts* pictured some 15 cars,

# Murray's Salvage Co.

## Las Vegas, Nevada

2. Early postwar Packard sedan could be restored yet, but a more likely fate is to continue as a source of parts for its luckier cousins. Behind the Packard is a '56 DeSoto Firedome four-door sedan, still wearing much of its original light blue and white finish.

## ABOUT THE YARD

Murray's Salvage Co., 6051 No. Hollywood, Las Vegas, NV 89115, phone 702-644-3324, is open normal business hours seven days a week (West Coast time zone). It's located to the north side of Las Vegas, just a few miles out of town. Dick Murray is the proprietor.

and when we revisited the yard just a short while ago, owner Dick Murray told us that all but one of those cars sold within a month or so after the article was published. Plus, hundreds of parts were sold off cars in the yard that were being parted out. Three different hobbyists from England ordered huge lots of parts off selected cars in the yard.

Nicer, more complete cars are generally sold as a whole, but most are parted out, a piece at a time. Four-door sedans, in particular, are parted out on arrival unless they're exceptionally clean and solid units. The rust-free sheet metal is incredibly well preserved.

Most of the cars in the yard were driven into their parking spots, and some could be back on the road with just a battery and some free gas. That's one reason Murray likes to sell cars as whole units, even though there is usually more money to be made in parting them out. ■

**3. Cadillac restorers and owners have already had their way with this 1947 four-door sedan, but its life as a parts car is far from over.**

**4. Inside the trunk of a '40 Dodge sedan, we found an old Chevrolet radiator and grille shell.**

**5. The '40 Dodge sedan with the Chevy radiator in the trunk has been pretty well picked over.**

6

6. Wow, a '54 Buick convertible? Well, not quite. This "convertible" was created by a conversion of a '54 Buick two-door hardtop.

7. Notchback '68 Ford Mustang appears at a distance to have been completely gutted, but on closer inspection, the drivetrain is at least partially there (no engine) and the interior is all there.

8. A shopper checks out a 1954 Ford Country Sedan station wagon, with overdrive. This little family hauler could be restored, and quite easily.

9. Parts hunters have just started on this '49 Plymouth Special Deluxe four-door sedan. There are plenty of parts remaining.

7

8

9

Photos courtesy Ecology Auto Wreckers
With a sign that looks more like the type you'd find at the entrance to a shopping center, Ecology Auto Wrecking beckons shoppers to its auto parts mall.

# Ecology Auto Wrecking

## Santa Fe Springs, California

# Ecology started it all … and now has 11,000 vehicles at 11 yards

by Phil Skinner

"One man's trash, is another man's treasure," and for Ecology Auto Parts, headquartered in Santa Fe Springs, Calif., this old saying is 100 percent accurate. To really understand how this multi-million-dollar business began one has to look back to someone being in the right place at the right time.

"It all started in the late 1960s when the current owners took over a landfill operation at the site of the Santa Fe Springs facility," said Mark Menadier, Ecology Auto Parts spokesman. "A couple of abandoned cars were left on the property, and some people came by and wanted to buy some parts off them. Before they knew it, the Ecology Auto Parts Company came into existence," he said.

Currently Ecology operates 11 parts yards scattered over Southern California, and even as far away as Phoenix, Arizona. Where Ecology really broke new ground was that the yard was a do-it-yourself facility, the first of its type in the world. By paying a nominal admission fee of $1 per person, you bring your own tools to the yard, and then search out the car holding the parts you need. There's no guessing as to what you are going to have to pay, as large boards are posted at the entrance with the basic prices, plus additional core charges, which are refundable.

Compared with regular parts yards, the savings can be from 50 to 80 percent. Doors, fenders, deck lids, and hoods are usually priced around $30 each, plus applicable core charges and sales tax. Still, with the same item costing more than $150 at a regular dismantler's facility, that can be quite a bargain.

There are a lot of other hidden benefits in coming to an Ecology Auto Parts yard, such as learning how to disassemble a car properly. With concealed screws and attaching clips providing a challenge in the removal of

Although Ecology is a do-it-yourself type of yard, there is help for pulling and transporting such major parts as engines, transmissions, and rear axles.

Each month, thousands of cars are cycled through Ecology's several yards, so no two visits are ever the same, and the time to buy your part is when you see it.

## ABOUT THE YARD

Ecology Auto Parts has its main offices at 13780 E. Imperial Highway, Santa Fe Springs, Calif. 90670. For "Parts on Request" or yard information, call 562-404-2277, (404-CARS), ext. 3340. Customers are not only allowed to roam the yard, but are encouraged to do so. An admission charge of $1 per person is applied, which is good for the entire day at that facility only. Prices and charges are generally posted at the front entrance to each yard. No one under 18 years old is allowed in the yard. Catering trucks are usually on site, and complimentary hand washing is provided.

body trim moldings, by practicing on one of their cars first in removing the needed parts, the customer can gain knowledge of automotive mysteries.

"We have worked hard to become customer friendly," said Menadier. "Little things like complimentary hand washing facilities, a service for which other yards charge up to $1.75, is one example."

At the Phoenix facility a number of special courtesies help there. Most people bring their tools in five-gallon buckets. As a free service the yard fills these buckets with ice, which serves two purposes; where temperatures can reach well over the century mark it keeps the tools cool, and as the ice melts the cool water can be poured over the parts to be removed to cool them off before being worked on. The Phoenix facility is actually divided into two separate sections, one for domestic tin, and the other for imports. Due to their locations being about a half-mile apart, a free "People & Parts" shuttle is provided.

Generally the age of the cars in these yards is at least 10 years old, and can date back to the 1960s. However, as the source of older cars has dried up over the years, Ecology Auto Parts has started to pull these potential collector items aside for sale to hobbyists who are looking for new projects.

"By going to each yard, you never know what you'll find," said Menadier, "and with the majority of our cars coming from California and Arizona, these are solid rust-free examples."

Rather than placing a set price on those saved chariots, interested parties make sealed bids for each car, with the usual minimum starting at $1,000.

Ecology's basic plan of operation is fairly simple. Through heavy local television and print advertising, people know that if they have an old car sitting in their driveway or backyard, one call to Ecology and it goes away, with a few dollars placed in their pocket.

A fleet of flat-bed tow trucks runs all over southern California daily, retrieving cars from all corners. About half of the vehicles that come to Ecology are brought in this way, with the other half coming from the more traditional way of insurance claim auctions, and police impound yards filled with abandoned cars.

After a car is brought to the yard, it has to be processed. Paperwork with the Department of Motor Vehicles has to be filed with each vehicle to make sure there are no liens or other problems. Due to ecological restrictions, certain parts have to be removed prior to the car being placed out on the rows for the customers. Most of those items are limited to emission control devices such as exhaust pipes and catalytic converters.

The stock in the yard is arranged by manufacturer, with all Chevrolet products in one place, while the rest of GM cars are grouped together. All Ford products are then placed in another section, with Chrysler and AMC products combined in another. Imports are gener-

ally placed by themselves.

In the early days of Ecology operations, the cars were placed in the yard "County Fair" style, i.e. put in rows as they were purchased. While this could make looking for the right car interesting, it did take a lot of time. By limiting the area of search, not only was money saved, but time too!

How long a car stays available for parts at Ecology depends on how fast stock is received. With limited room in the impound yard, once a car is cleared, and enough units of a similar model are available to make a new row, they are placed in the yard. All day long, giant fork-lifts pick up the stripped hulk, while a crew cleans up the loose parts, and the row is readied for a fresh stock of parts contributors.

Ecology Auto Parts is a do-it-yourself facility, but you are not totally alone. Another benefit provided to customers that can be very helpful is an Interchange Service. Often a person might be looking for a mechanical item, like an alternator for a Mustang. By going to the Information Center, available at each yard, the Interchange Service may be able to find that Mustang's alternator under the hood of a Mercury Monarch, or even an old Pinto.

More recently, Ecology has instituted a "Parts on Request" program. This is designed to operate on a similar system to regular parts yards, where the customer places an inquiry. They search the stock of their 11 yards, and if the part is found a price is quoted which includes removal and delivery to the customer's home, or shop, or wherever the part is needed. Should Ecology not have the requested part, it has access to a nationwide parts line to aid in the search. For those customers who can't make it to the yard to pick up the parts, shipping is also available.

Recently, Ecology Auto Parts has started to take part in several vintage vehicle events in and around southern California. It is the named sponsor to the

very successful Hi-Performance Swap Meet held monthly at the Long Beach Veterans Stadium, and also supports Ray Taylor's monthly Parts Exchange and Car Corral held on the grounds of San Diego's Jack Murphy Stadium.

"We are also sponsoring a new quarterly swap meet," Menadier told Cars & Parts. "We had our first event in August 1998, and are planning to present one every three months at Hollywood Park in Inglewood."

Of course, half the fun of buying parts is coming to where the cars are. Generally each yard operates seven days a week, opening at 7:30 a.m., closing at 6 p.m. during the summer, and 5 p.m. the rest of the year. You have to bring your own tools, and transactions can be made with cash or credit cards. There are even ATM machines on site. If you are bringing a part to the yard for comparison, be sure to point this out at the entrance gate so it can be marked. Tool boxes are inspected going in and going out. With a hand stamp, you can have access to the yard all day long for one admission price. Children under 18 are not allowed to enter the yard, due to safety and insurance reasons.

Most of the cars we found on our last journey to the Santa Fe Springs facility were from the mid-1970s, to the early 1990s, with a few dating back to the late 1960s. At any one time, as many as 11,500 cars may be available at the 11 yards. In addition to Santa Fe Springs, and Phoenix, Arizona, the other Southern California locations include Wilmington, Monterey Park, Rialto, Adelanto, Oceanside, two locations in Chula Vista, San Diego, and the newest site, Lancaster.

Since Ecology Auto Parts started with those few abandoned cars, it has probably disposed of more than two million vehicles, vehicles that would have gone to the crusher or shredder without giving thousands an opportunity to save a few choice parts at a substantial savings. ∎

**One of the customer services offered at the Ecology center is a complimentary hand washing center, a most welcome convenience.**

# Salvage Yard Directory

## ALASKA

**Binder's Auto Restoration:** 1 Mile Mayd Rd., P.O. Box 1144, Palmer, Alaska 99645. Phone 907-745-4670. Otto Binder. Hours by appointment only. 1960-90s Cadillac only mail order salvage yard. No part too small. SASE with parts list.

## ARIZONA

**Art Coffer Auto Dismantlers., Inc.:** 3127 W. Broadway Rd., Phoenix, Ariz. 85041. Phone 602-276-7377. Tom Taber. Hours Mon.-Fri. 8 a.m.-5 p.m., Sat. 8 a.m.-2 p.m. Customers may browse yard with supervision. Specializes in Chrysler, Plymouth and Dodge from 1960 to 1991. No Ford or GM. Used cars and trucks. Founded in 1966. Approximately 500-600 vehicles in yard.

**Boneyard Stan:** Stanley Jones, 218 N. 69 Ave., Phoenix, Ariz. 85043. Phone 602-936-8045. Normal business hours seven days a week. Arizona Pontiacs our specialty. American cars and parts 1940s to 1980s, shipping and references worldwide. Hobby since 1975.

**Carpieces:** P.O. Box 15548, Phoenix, Ariz. 85060-5548. Phone 602-376-1561; Fax 602-852-0442. Hours 7 days a week, almost 24 hours. Postwar American Western rustfree sheetmetal, chrome, glass, options. Nearly $1M inventory. Mail order only. Locator service.

**Chi-town Auto Wrecking:** 2935 W. Broadway, Phoenix, Ariz. 85041. Phone 602-268-2400, 602-268-5637. Dan and Janet Rush, owners. Hours 8 a.m.-6 p.m. Mon.-Sat., Sun. 9 a.m.-3 p.m.

**Desert Valley Auto Parts:** 22500 N. 21st Ave., Phoenix, Ariz. 85027. Phone 1-800-905-8024; Fax 602-582-9141; www.dvap.com. Hours Mon.-Fri. 8 a.m.-5:30 p.m., Sat. 8 a.m.-2 p.m. Over 30 acres and over 5,000 cars and trucks from the 1940s through the 1970s for parts or restoration.

**Global Auto Parts Connection:** P.O. Box 15548, Phoenix, Ariz. 86060. Phone 602-376-1561. Almost 24 hours, 7 days. Rust free Western used auto parts. Post war GM, Ford, Chrysler, Lincoln. Locator service. Access to over 100,000 parts cars.

**Hidden Valley Auto Parts:** Jeff Hoctor, 21046 N. Rio Bravo, Maricopa, Ariz. 85239. Phone 602-252-2122, 252-6137; Fax 602-258-0951. Hours Mon.-Fri. 8 a.m.-5 p.m., Sat. 9 a.m.-3 p.m. Over 80 acres of used auto parts. Send specific list w/SASE. Ship worldwide. In business 32 years.

**Speedway Automotive:** 2300 West Broadway, Phoenix, Ariz. 85041. Phone 602-276-0090. Hours Mon.-Fri. 8:30 a.m.-5:30 p.m., Sat. 9 a.m.-3 p.m. Customers may browse yard. Mail-order service. Specializes in 1961 and newer Buicks. Many Grand Nationals and GS'. Over 600 Buicks in stock. In business 18 years.

**Wiseman's Auto Salvage:** 900 West Cottonwood Lane, Casa Grande, Ariz. 85222. Phone 520-836-7960. Ron Wiseman. Hours Mon.-Fri. 8 a.m.-5:30 p.m., Sat. 9 a.m.-1:30 p.m. Approximately 3,000 cars and trucks from '20s-'70s. Browsers welcome. We ship. In business since early '60s

## ARKANSAS

**Big Ben's Used Cars & Salvage:** Highway 79 East, Fordyce, Ark. 71742. Phone 501-352-7423. Benny or Sherry Roark. Hours Mon.-Thurs., 8 a.m.-5 p.m., Fri. 8 a.m.-6 p.m., Sat. 8 a.m.-1 p.m. Customers may browse yard. Specializes in all makes from the '60s and '70s, particularly Chryslers. Approximately 1,500 vehicles in yard. In scrap iron and metals business.

**Vintage Auto Salvage:** Ed Summar, 7411 Hwy. 367N, Bradford, Ark. 72020. Phone 501-344-8370. Hours Tues.-Fri. 9 a.m.-5 p.m.; Sat. 9 a.m.-4 p.m. We carry cars and trucks from the 1950s and '60s. But have some as old as 1926 and as late as 1978. We sell parts or whole vehicles.

## CALIFORNIA

**Aase Bros. Inc.:** 701 E. Cypress St., Anaheim, Calif. 92805. Phone 714-956-2419; 1-800-444-7444. Dave or Dennis Aase. Hours Mon.-Fri. 8:30 a.m.-5:30 p.m. Mail-order service available. Yard specializes in Porsche and Mercedes. Approximately 200 vehicles in the yard. In business over 22 years.

**Allchevy Auto Parts:** 4999 Vanden Rd., Vacaville, Calif. 95687. Phone 707-437-5466; Fax 707-437-6821. Billy Marks. Hours Mon.-Fri., 8:30 a.m.-5:30 p.m. Customers may browse yard. Mail-order service. Specializes in Chevy cars and trucks, 1955-93. Approximately 200 vehicles in yard. Computerized inventory, parts locating system nationally. In business over 9 years.

**Best Deal Inc.:** 8171 Monroe, Stanton, Calif. 90680. Phone 1-800-354-9202, 714-995-0081. John Waner. Hours Mon.-Fri. 8:30 a.m.-5 p.m., Sat. 9 a.m.-3 p.m. New and used parts and accessories for Porsche enthusiasts. Mail-order service. Catalog available. In business since 1975.

**Capital Auto Parts:** 15326 S. Figueroa, Gardena, Calif. 90248. Los Angeles area. Phone 213-323-4242.

**Crossroads Classic Mustang:** 12421 Riverside Ave., Mira Loma, Calif. 91752. Phone 714-986-6789, 1-800-Giddy-Up (catalog). Paul Nusbaum or Norm Stepnick. Hours Mon.-Fri. 8 a.m.-5 p.m., Sat. 8:30 a.m.-2 p.m. Customers may browse yard. Mail-order service. Specializes in 1964 1/2 and up Mustangs. Approximately 250 Mustangs in yard. New and reproduced parts, rebuilt parts. In business since 1967.

**E & H Auto Wreckers:** 595 Trade Zone Blvd., Milpitas, Calif. 95035. Phone 408-262-4500.

**Ecology Auto Wrecking:** 13780 E. Imperial Highway, Santa Fe Springs, Calif. 90670 (main office). Phone 562-404-2277 or 404-CARS, ext. 3340. Customers are allowed to roam the yard, bring your own tools. Operates 11 parts yards scattered over southern California. Nominal admission fee of $1.

**Gilly's Auto Wreckers:** 2561 Blacks Lane, Placerville, Calif. 95667. Phone 916-622-4052, toll-free 1-888-622-4052; ianjhunt @gillys.com. Hours Mon-Sat. 8 a.m.-5 p.m. Approximately 600 vehicles. Specializes in 1972 and older vehicles.

**Kalend's Auto Wrecking:** 8237 E. Hwy. 26, Stockton, Calif. 95215. Phone 209-931-0929. George DeYoung or Ken Aman. Hours Mon.-Fri. 8 a.m.-5 p.m., Sat. 9 a.m.-2 p.m. Mail orders accepted. Customers may browse yard. Specializes in 1980 to 1990 all makes cars and parts, domestic and foreign. Approximately 400 vehicles in yard. In business over 40 years.

**Lee's Auto:** Route 1, Box 1632, Orland, Calif. 95963. Lee Carter. Open normal business hours. Stocks 300-plus vehicles, with most older than 1970. Many commercial vehicles in the 5.5-acre yard, including a number of restorable units. In business under current management for over 10 years.

**L&R Butler Auto Dismantler:** 5008 Patterson Ave., Perris, Calif. 92531. Five acres of '50s & '60s cars. Mostly Chrysler, Dodge, Desoto, Plymouth, also Hudson. Many misc. parts from '20s, '30s, '40s cars. Hundreds of brake drum starters & generators.

**Mather's Auto Dismantlers, Inc.:** 4095 Happy Lane, Sacramento, Calif. 95827. Phone 916-366-8211.

**M.A.T.S.:** 701 Straugh Rd., Rio Linda, Calif. 95673. Phone 916-991-3033. Darin Moore. Hours Mon.-Fri. 9 a.m.-5 p.m., Sat. 9 a.m.-3 p.m. Inventory list available. Customers may browse yard. Mail orders accepted. Specializes in 1948-85 pickups and cars up to and including 1975. Approximately 1,500 vehicles. In business over 7 years.

**Memory Lane:** Tony Martinez, 11311 Pendleton St., Sun Valley, Calif. 91352. Phone 818-504-3341, 1-800-281-9273; Fax 818-768-2613; www.oldautoparts.com. Hours Mon.-Fri. 8 a.m.-5 p.m., Sat. 8 a.m.-4 p.m. Collectible and muscle car parts. Specializing in 1940s-70s cars and trucks.

**Papke Enterprises, Inc.:** Bill Papke, 17202 Gothard St., Huntington Beach, Calif. 92647. Phone 714-843-6969 (shop). Hours Mon.-Sat. by appointment only. Inventory list available. Mail-order service. Specializes in 1949-51 Mercurys and Fords. Many other Ford and Mercury parts, chrome accessories and custom items. In business over 19 years.

**Pearson's Auto Dismantling & Used Cars:** 2343 Hwy. 49, Mariposa, Calif. 95338. Phone 209-742-7442. A.G. Pearson. Hours Wed.-Fri. 9 a.m.-6 p.m., Sat. 9 a.m.-5 p.m. Mail-order service for small items. Customers may browse yard. Specializes in all makes and models of '40s, '50s, and '60s. No classics. Approximately 1,500 vehicles in yard. In business over 38 years.

**Pearsonville Auto Wrecking & Hubcap Store:** 236 Pearson Rd., Pearsonville, Calif. 93527. Phone 619-377-4585; Fax 619-377-5446. Parts shipping available. Hubcap capitol of the world. Several thousand vehicles, from post-war on up.

**Romo Auto Wrecking:** Ron Romo, 4625 No. Golden State Blvd., Fresno, Calif. 93722. Phone 209-275-4823. Hours Tues.-Sat. 8 a.m.-5 p.m.; Sun. 9 a.m.-4 p.m., closed on Mon. One family ownership for over 75 years. Over 1,500 cars and trucks from the early '80s on back. 1930s, 40s, 50s and 60s are the house specialty.

**Tressar's Auto Salvage:** 120 S. Amphlett's Blvd., San Mateo, Calif. 94401. Phone 415-343-6754.

**Turner's Auto Wrecking:** 4248 S. Willow Ave., Fresno, Calif. 93725. Phone 209-237-0918. Mail-order service. Old car parts from 1940s to 1970s. In business approximately 40 years.

**Withers Auto Wrecking:** 138AAA Rt. 2, Tulelake, Calif. 96134. Phone 916-664-2204, 541-884-3289. Call for hours. Parts from teens to '80s, including WWII parts. Many old restorable complete vehicles for sale. Entire yard for sale.

**Z & Z Auto Salvage:** 233 N. Lemon, Orange, Calif. 92666. Phone 714-997-2200. Hours normal hours weekdays, weekends by appointment only. Specializing in Camaros & Firebirds, and offering restorations. In business over 19 years.

## COLORADO

**American Auto Salvage:** Butch Jarvis, 2773 D Road, Grand Junction, Colo. 81501. Phone 970-243-0373. Approximately 550 cars. Customers may browse yard. Towing available. In business since 1955.

**Ernest's Auto Wrecking:** Ernest Quintana, P.O. Box 6, Capulin, Colo. 81124. Phone 719-274-5224. Hours Mon.-Fri. 9 a.m.-8 p.m., Sat. 8 a.m.-5 p.m., Sun. by appointment only. Escorted browsing. In business since 1968.

**Eddie Paul:** 9150 Boone Road, Yoder, Colo. 80864. Phone 719-478-2723. Hours Mon.-Fri. 8 a.m.-9 p.m., Sat. 8 a.m.-9 p.m. by appointment only. Customers may browse yard. Mail-order service. Approximately 35 vehicles in yard. In business over 16 years.

**Martin Supply & Salvage Yard:** 8405 U.S. Hwy. 34, Windsor, Colo. 80550. Phone 303-686-2460.

**Morgan Auto Parts:** 722 Kennie Rd., Pueblo, Colo. 81001. Phone 303-545-1702. Dennis Morgan. Hours Mon.-Fri. 8 a.m.-5 p.m., Sat. 8 a.m.-1 p.m. Customers may browse yard. Mail-order service. Specializes in all makes and models. Approximately 450 vehicles in yard. In business over 30 years.

**Speedway Auto Wrecking:** Roland Cochran or Bill Renoad, 4394 Weld County Rd., No. 12, Erie, Colo. 80516. Phone 303-893-1153, Fax 303-833-0332. Hours Mon.-Fri. 8 a.m.-5:30 p.m., Sat. 8 a.m.-5 p.m. 1940s thru 1980s parts for cars and trucks.

**West 29th Auto Inc.:** 3200 W. 29th St., Pueblo, Colo. 81003. Phone 719-543-4247, 719-543-4249. Glenn Kittinger. Hours Tues.-Sat. 8 a.m.-5 p.m. Mail-order service. 80 acres, 30-year accumulation, old to new merchandise, all makes. Approximately 4,000 vehicles in yard. In business over 30 years.

**Woller Auto Parts, Inc.:** Don Woller, 8227 Road SS, Lamar, Colo. 81052. Phone 719-336-2108. Hours Mon.-Fri. 8 a.m.-5:30 p.m., Sat. 8 a.m.-noon. Mail-order service. Specializes in 1955-84 models, mostly domestic and pickups. Approximately 4,000 vehicles in yard. Offers paint, body, glass and mechanical work, etc. In business over 20 years.

## CONNECTICUT

**Stewart's Used Auto Parts:** Gary Stewart, P.O. Box 352, New Hartford, Conn. 06057. Phone 860-379-7541; Fax 860-379-8933. Hours Mon.-Fri. 8 a.m.-5 p.m., Sat. 8 a.m.-2 p.m. Mail order. Browsers are escorted. In business since 1949.

**Leo Winakor & Sons, Inc.:** 470 Forsyth Rd., Salem, Conn. 06415. Phone 860-859-0471. Hours Sat. 10 a.m.-3 p.m., Sun. 10 a.m.-2 p.m., or by appointment. Mail orders accepted. Customers may browse yard. Specializes in all makes and models from 1930 to 1981. Parts, complete vehicles and restorables. Approximately 1,500 vehicles.

**Mt. Tobe Auto Parts:** Mt. Tobe Auto Parts, R.F.D. 1, Plymouth, Conn. 06782. Yard is located on Mt. Tobe Rd. Phone 203-753-0332.

# FLORIDA

**Holder's Auto Salvage:** 12404 Highway 231, Youngstown, Fla. 32466. Phone 904-722-4993. Carlos Holder. Hours Mon.-Sat. 8 a.m.-5 p.m. Specializing in thirties thru seventies cars and truck parts. We also sell whole vehicles. We ship anywhere and will deliver whole vehicles. In business over 10 years.

**J and B Auto Parts, Inc.:** 17105 E. Hwy. 50, Orlando, Fla. 32820. Phone 305-568-2131. N.C. or N.L. Horton Sr. Hours Mon.-Fri. 8 a.m.-5:30 p.m., Sat.-Sun. 8 a.m.-4 p.m. Mail orders accepted. Customers may browse. Specializes in all years and makes American and foreign, cars and trucks. Approximately 1,500 vehicles in yard. Firm has radiator shop, service department, installs glass and has towing service. In business over 39 years.

**Old Gold Cars & Parts:** Rt. 2 Box 1133, Old Town, Fla. 32680. Phone 904-542-8085. Steven or Shannon. Hours Mon.-Fri. 8 a.m.-6 p.m. Mail order services. Yard specializes in 1948-78 American make only. Approximately 3,500 vehicles in yard. In business over six years.

**Sunrise Auto Sales and Salvage:** Rt. 3, Box 6, Aero Ave., Lake City, Fla. 32055. Phone 904-755-1810; Fax 904-755-1855. William Lockwood. Hours Mon.-Fri. 8 a.m.-5:30 p.m., Sat. 8 a.m.-1 p.m. Customers may browse yard. Mail-order service. Specializes in '40s through early '70s cars and trucks. A few '30s. Over 1,000 autos. In business over four years.

**Umatilla Auto Salvage:** 19714 Saltsdale Rd., Umatilla, Fla. 32784. Phone 904-669-6363. Thomas Lee. Hours Mon.-Fri. 9 a.m.-5 p.m., Sat. 8 a.m.-12 noon. Customers may browse yard. Mail-order service. Yard specializes in '50s through '70s, all makes, a few imports and luxury. Approximately 1,000 vehicles in the yard. In business over 10 years.

# GEORGIA

**Fiat Lancia Heaven:** 1111 Via Bayless, Marietta, Ga. 30066. Phone (orders) 1-800-241-1446, information 404-928-1446. Hours Mon.-Fri. 8 a.m.-5:30 p.m. Exclusively Fiat and Lancia Beta automobiles 1953-1988.

**Clark's Auto Parts:** Hwy. 23 near Georgia Highway Patrol barracks, Helena, Ga. 31037. Firm has nearly 2,500 vehicles, including cars and light trucks from '30s to late '70s.

**Collins Auto Salvage, Inc.:** Gerald Collins, 574 Blackstock Rd., Auburn, Ga. 30011. Phone 770-963-2650. Hours Mon.-Thurs. 8 a.m.-6 p.m., Fri. 8 a.m.-5 p.m., Sat. 8 a.m.-4 p.m. Maintains an inventory of 500-1000 older cars on its 25-acre yard. In business since 1969.

**Embee Parts:** 4000 Lee Rd., Smyrna, Ga. 30080. Phone 404-434-5686. George Wolfes. Hours Mon.-Fri. 9 a.m.-6 p.m., Sat. 9 a.m.-noon. Customers may browse yard. Mail-order service. Specializes in 1934-88 Mercedes. Approximately 500 vehicles in yard. In business over 10 years.

**H.L. Hodges Salvage Yard & Used Parts:** Hugh L. Hodges, Jr., 3995 Treadwell Bridge Rd., Monroe, Ga. 30656. Phone 770-267-3461. Hours Mon.-Sat. 9 a.m.-4 p.m. Approximately 1,200-1,500 cars ranging from the '40s into the '70s. In business since the early '50s.

**Old Car City, USA:** Dean or Ed, 3098 Hwy. 411 NE, P.O. Box 480, White, Ga. 30184. Phone 404-382-6141. Hours M-T-Th-F 8 a.m.-5 p.m., W-S 8 a.m.-12 p.m. Charge for tours. All American cars, pickups, 1918-1972 models. Over 4,000 vehicles in yard. In business since 1931, same family.

**Park's Used Auto Parts:** Friendship Rd., Eatonton, Ga. 31024. Richard Park. Phone 706-485-9905; 706-485-4511. Hours 2 p.m.-6 p.m., all day Sat. Mail-order service. Specializing in muscle, antique and street rod cars & parts. Also trucks and mobile home axles.

**Weatherley's Old Cars & Parts:** Owen Weatherley, 414 Russell Cemetery Rd., Winder, Ga. 30680. Phone 770-867-3963. Hours Saturday only, weekdays call ahead. A collection of 150-200 old cars.

# IDAHO

**Classic Auto Parts:** Mike Waller, 18090 Hwy. 95, Hayden Lake, Idaho 83835. Phone 208-762-8080. Hours Mon.-Fri. 9 a.m.-3 p.m.

**Highway 30 Auto Wrecking:** 960 Sunset Strip, Highway 30 W, Mount Home, Idaho 83647. Phone 208-587-4429. Cort Braithwaite, owner. Hours Mon.-Fri. 9 a.m.-5 p.m., Sat. 9 a.m.-1 p.m.

**Hopkins Antique Autos and Parts:** 24833 Highway 30, Caldwell, Idaho 83605. Phone 208-459-2877.

**L. & L. Classic Auto:** 2742 State Highway 46, Wendell, Idaho 83355. Phone 208-536-6606.

**Morris' Antique and Classic Cars & Parts:** Indian Valley, Idaho 83632. Phone 208-256-4313. Lynn Morris, owner.

**Vintage Automotive:** P.O. Box 958, 2290 N. 18th E., Mtn. Home, Idaho 83647. Phone 208-587-3743. Jim Hines. Hours Mon.-Fri. 9 a.m.-6 p.m., Sat. 10 a.m.-5 p.m. Customers may browse yard. Specializes in all makes prior to 1970. Specializing in Metropolitan. Good stock of new parts for pre-'70 cars, trucks, and equipment. Approximately 1000 vehicles in yard. Sand blasting. Locator service. In business over 23 years.

# ILLINOIS

**Ace Auto Salvage:** Hwy. 51, Tonica, Ill. 61370. Phone 815-442-8224, 815-442-

8225. Mitchell Urban. Hours Mon.-Fri. 8 a.m.-5 p.m., Sat. 8 a.m.-noon. Customers may browse yard. Specializes in antique, collectible, convertibles, and muscle cars. Approximately 4,000 vehicles in yard. In business over 29 years.

**B.C. Automotive, Inc.:** Steve Slocum, 2809 Damascus, Zion, Ill. 60099. Phone 312-746-8056. Hours Mon.-Sat. 8:30 a.m.-5 p.m. Customers may browse yard. Mail-order service available. Specializes in 1960-82 domestic and 1970-84 foreign. Approximately 600 vehicles in yard. Towing services. In business over 10 years.

**Bryant's Auto Parts:** Wayne and Pat Bryant, RR 1, Westville, Ill. 61883. Phone 217-267-2124 or 1-800-252-5087. Hours Mon.-Fri. 8 a.m.-5 p.m., Sat. 8 a.m.-noon. Inventory list available. Customers are not permitted to pull parts. Mail-order service. Vehicles available as far back as 1939. Approximately 3,700 vehicles in yard. In business since 1959.

**Casner Motor Co.:** Christa K. Hjort, RR 1, Box 217, Oakley, Ill. 62552. Phone 217-864-2162. Located four miles east of Decatur on U.S. Rt. 36. Hours Mon., Tues., Wed., Fri. 9 a.m.-4 p.m., Sat. 9 a.m.-noon. Older model parts salvage yard, all makes. Lots of NOS left. Built in 1928 as a Ford dealership.

**E & J Used Auto & Truck Parts:** P.O. Box 6007, 315-31st Ave., Rock Island, Ill. 61204. Phone 309-788-7686, 1-800-728-7686. Rick, Jon, Marc or Tiny. Hours Mon.-Fri. 8 a.m.-4:30 p.m., Sat. 8 a.m.-1 p.m. Customers may browse yard. Specializes in all American and foreign cars and trucks from 1937-93. Mail-order service. Approximately 3,500 vehicles in yard. In business over 42 years.

**Gus Miller:** P.O. Box 604, Heyworth, Ill. 61745. Phone 309-473-2979. Hours by appointment only. Over 500 cars from the '40s and '50s, some '60s. Many orphan makes. No mail order.

**Savanna Auto Parts:** R.R. 1 Box 88, Thomson, Ill. 61285. Phone 815-273-2541. Sylvester McWorthy, Prop. Collection of older parts 1940 thru 1960. Some older, no body parts except glass, wheels, springs, axles, transmissions, carburetors, magnetos, mufflers, tailpipes, generators, starters, glass bottom channels, voltage regulators, much more. Need something inquire.

# INDIANA

**Auto Heaven:** Chuck Forney, 103 W. Allen Street, Bloomington, Ind. 47401. Phone 812-332-9401, 1-800-777-0297. Hours Mon.-Fri. 8:30 a.m.-5:30 p.m., Sat. 8:30 a.m.-noon. Customers may browse yard. Mail-order service available. Approximately 700 to 1,000 vehicles in yard. In business over 14 years.

**BSIA Mustang Supply.:** 0278 S. 700 E., Millcreek, Ind. 46365. Phone 219-369-9193. William S. Chalik or Carol M. Chalik. Hours Mon.-Sun. by appointment only. Customers may browse yard. Mail-order service. Specializes in 1964 1/2-1973

Mustangs, 1928-31 Model A Fords. Approximately 100 vehicles. Sales of new and reproduction parts. In business since 1978.

**Canfield Motors:** 22-24 Main St., New Waverly, Ind. 46961. Phone 219-722-3230. Robert Canfield. Hours Mon.-Fri. 8 a.m.-4 p.m., Sat. by appointment only. Specializes in 1940-up American made vehicles. Approximately 1,000 vehicles in yard. In business 40 years.

**Raef's Auto Body:** Gary Raef, 9701 E. Co. Rd. 600 South, Selma, Ind. 47383. Phone 765-774-4311, Fax 765-774-3511. Hours Mon.-Fri. 8 a.m.-5 p.m., Sat. flexible. Main business auto body work. Only complete cars are sold. Approximately 40 cars and trucks.

**Robinson's Auto Sales:** 200 New York Ave., New Castle, Ind. 47362. Phone 317-529-7603. Brent or Charlie Robinson. Hours Mon.-Fri. 8 a.m.-6 p.m., Sat. 8 a.m.-4 p.m. Customers may browse yard. Mail-order service. Specializes in Cadillacs, Corvairs, 1960-70. Approximately 25-30 vehicles in yard. Many NOS parts 1950-60, wheel covers and hubcaps 1940 on up. In business over 47 years.

**H. Shore & Sons Garage:** Gene and Russell Shore, P.O. Box 96, Modoc, Ind. 47358. Phone 765-853-5141. Hours Mon.-Fri. 6:30 a.m.-6:30 p.m., Sat. 7 a.m.-6 p.m. Over 400 cars. Complete mechanical service. Customers are allowed to pull parts. In business since 1933.

**Webb's Classic Auto Parts:** Jim Webb, 5084 West State Road 114, Huntington, Ind. 46750. Phone 219-344-1714; Fax 219-344-1754; http://user.huntington.in.us/jwebb. Hours Mon.-Fri. 8 a.m.-5 p.m. Specializing in AMC, Rambler auto recycling. NOS, used, reproduction parts, technical service manuals, walk in or mail-order service. UPS shipping.

**Wright's Auto Service:** 102 S. Shelby, Indianapolis, Ind. 46202. Phone 317-638-4482. Arthur or Edith Wells. Hours Mon.-Fri. 9 a.m.-5 p.m. Mail orders accepted with prepaid check. Specializes in parts from 1930 to 1959 and cars of early vintage. Services include repairs to older cars (transmissions, motors and brakes). Many rebuilt items available. No body work. Doing business since 1939.

# IOWA

**Becker's Auto Salvage:** Mike Becker, Hwy. 30 West, Atkins, Iowa 52206. Phone 319-446-7141. Hours Mon.-Fri. 8 a.m.-5 p.m., Sat. 8 a.m.-noon. Customers may browse yard. Mail-order service. Specializes in AMCs, Fords, Studebakers, Edsels, Chevys, and more. Yard consists of 10 acres. In business over 26 years.

**Kelsey Auto Salvage:** Rt. 2, Iowa Falls, Iowa 50126. Phone 515-648-3066. Located on 00 Avenue southeast of Iowa Falls, in north central Iowa. Take Rocksylvania Ave., turn right on 00 Avenue; the yard will be two miles away. Dean or Chuck. Hours

Tues.-Fri. 8 a.m.-5 p.m., Sat. 8 a.m.-noon. Mail orders accepted. Customers may browse yard. Specializes in American cars from 1965 to 1980. 250 vehicles in yard. Started in 1974.

**Meier Auto Salvage Inc.:** RR 1, Box 6L, Sioux City, Iowa 51108. Phone 712-239-1344. Dan and Mike Goosmann. Hours Mon.-Fri. 8 a.m.-5 p.m., Sat. 8:30 a.m.-4 p.m. Inventory list available. Customers may browse yard. Mail-order service. Specializes in 1935-65 (250), 1965-88 (700). Approximately 1,000 vehicles in yard. In business over 25 years.

**Norm's Antique Auto Supply:** 1921 Hickory Grove Rd., Davenport, Iowa 52804. Phone 319-322-8388. Norm Miller. Hours Mon.-Friday 9 a.m.-5 p.m., Sat. 9 a.m.-noon. Customers may browse yard. Mail-order service. Specializes in 1917-69 Fords, 1923-53 Chevys, 1929-55 Chrysler products, 1923-32 Durant products, 1935-52 Packards, and GM products. Approximately 150 vehicles in yard. Offers speedometer, cable, starter, generator and distributor services, vacuum tanks rebuilt. In business over 26 years.

**North End Wrecking, Inc.:** 55 West 32nd St., Dubuque, Iowa 52001. Phone 319-556-0044. Don Dick. Hours Mon.-Fri. 8 a.m.-5 p.m. Mail-order service. Miscellaneous late-model parts only. Approximately 1,200 vehicles in yard. In business over 40 years.

**Parmer Studebaker Sales:** 408 S. Lincoln, Van Wert, Iowa 50262. Phone 515-445-5692. Eddie L. Parmer. Call anytime, appointments only. Customers may browse yard. Mail-order service. Many new parts in stock; still buying new used parts, locating service. Specializes in Studebakers only, 1946-66 autos, 1946-64 trucks. Approximately 70-80 vehicles in yard, others dismantled in bins. In business since 1971.

**Ron's Auto Salvage:** R.R. 2, Box 54, Allison, Iowa 50602. Phone 319-267-2871. Ronald Saathoff. Hours Mon.-Fri. 8 a.m.-5 p.m., Sat. 8 a.m.-noon. Customers may browse yard. Mail-order service. Specializes in all makes 1949-85 cars and pickups. Approximately 2,000 vehicles in yard. In business over 25 years.

**Terry's Auto Parts:** Box 131, Granville, Iowa 51022. Phone 712-727-3273. Hours Mon.-Fri. 8 a.m.-5 p.m., Sat. 8 a.m.-1 p.m. Customers may browse yard. Mail orders accepted. Specializes in 1940-84 Buicks, including 1963-84 Rivieras with all assembly and misc. body parts available. Approximately 100 vehicles in yard. In business over 29 years.

**Vander Haag's, Inc.:** 3809 4th Ave. West, Spencer, Iowa 51301-2082. Phone 712-262-7000; Fax 712-262-7421. John C. Vander Haag. Hours 8 a.m.-5 p.m. Specialize in trucks used 1940-96. Parts all years. Also new, rebuilt and new take off parts. Flyer available. In business since 1939.

# KANSAS

**"Easy Jack" & Sons Auto Parts:** 2725 South Milford Lake Rd., Junction City, Kan. 66441-8446. Phone 913-238-7541, 913-238-7161. Easy Jack, Joe or Jamin. Located 6 miles west of Junction City, I-70, exit 290. Hours Mon.-Fri. 8 a.m.-5:30 p.m., Sat. 8 a.m.-2 p.m. Mail-order service. Large collection of antique and collector-type cars from 1912 through 1982, most makes. Antique new and used parts. Services include used cars, towing, storage, shop work and parts location. In business since 1963.

**Edmonds Old Car Parts:** P.O. Box 303, 307 East Pearl, McLouth, Kan. 66054. Phone 913-796-6529, 913-796-6529 (home). Jim Edmonds. Hours Mon.-Fri. 5 p.m.-9 p.m., Sat. 9 a.m.-5 p.m. Open by appointment only. Customers may browse yard. Mail-order service. Specializes in Chevrolets from 1928-57, Chevy pickups from 1928-66. Approximately 35 vehicles in yard.

**Jim's Auto Sales:** Rt. 2, Inman, Kan. 67546. Phone 316-585-6648. James D. White. Hours Mon.-Sat. 9 a.m.-5 p.m. Open Sun. by appointment. Mail orders accepted. Customers may browse yard. Firm specializes in Studebakers 1935-66. Over 250 cars in stock. Has Mopars from the late '30s to mid-'70s, and a few Ford and GM products of the '40s to early '70s. NOS Studebaker parts. In business over 25 years.

**Bob Lint Motor Shop:** Bob Lint, P.O. Box 87, 101 Main, Danville, Kan. 67036. Phone 316-962-5247. Hours Mon.-Fri. 9 a.m.-5 p.m., Sat. 1 p.m.-5 p.m. Thousands of cars and pickup truck parts. Radiators, motors, wheels, fenders, hoods, doors, hubcaps, transmissions, rear ends, etc. In business for 45 years at this location.

# KENTUCKY

**Antique Auto Shop:** Terry Kesselring, 603 Lytle Ave., Elsmere, Ky. 41018. Phone 606-342-8363. Hours Mon.-Fri. 8 a.m.-5 p.m.

**Nolley Auto Sales, Inc.:** Charles Nolley, South Central Ave., Campbellsville, Ky. 42718. Phone 502-465-2306 shop, 502-465-4413 home. Prefer to sell whole units, either as restorable vehicles or parts cars, but some parts can be acquired individually off selected units.

**R.C. Van Cleave & Son Used Cars & Trucks:** 344 Salem Church Rd., Campbellsville, Ky. 42718. Phone 502-465-2329. Open by appointment. Randall Van Cleave. Prefer to sell whole units, either as restorable vehicles or parts cars, but some parts can be acquired individually off selected units.

# LOUISIANA

**Fannaly's Auto Exchange:** Marion Fannaly, P.O. Box 23, Ponchatoula, La. 70454. Phone 504-386-3714. Open by appointment only. Over 400 parts cars, 25 or more restorable cars, considerable inventory NOS, various makes. In business since 1954.

## MARYLAND

**Chuck's Used Auto Parts:** 4722 St. Barnabas Rd., Marlow Heights, Md. 20748. Phone 301-423-0007. Chuck Ryan or Chuck Pounds. Hours Mon.-Fri. 8 a.m.-5 p.m., Sat. 8 a.m.-2 p.m. Mail-order service. Specializes in all Corvettes, late model GM cars and trucks. Car sales of rebuildable vehicles. Parts location service. Approximately 250 vehicles in yard. In business over 12 years.

**The Mercedes Connection:** Robert Neuberth, 3707 Cassen Rd., Randallstown, Md. 21133. Phone: 410-922-1410; Fax 410-466-3566; tmcpub@jagunet.com. Hours Mon.-Sat. 9 a.m.-6 p.m. Dedicated to the preservation of older Mercedes-Benz cars. We carry parts cars from 1958-80, all models.

**Petry's Junk Yard, Inc.:** 800 Gorsuch Rd., Westminster, Md. 21157. Phone 301-876-3233, 301-848-8590. Tom Runaldue, Tom Petry or Harry. Hours Mon.-Sat. 8 a.m.-5 p.m. Open Sundays by appointment only. Inventory list available. Customers may browse yard. Mail orders accepted. Specializes in all makes and models of the '40s through the '70s. Approximately 400 to 500 vehicles in yard. Towing services. In business over 25 years.

**Smith Brothers Auto Parts:** 2316 Snydersburg Rd., Hampstead, Md. 21074. Phone 301-239-8514, 301-374-6781. Ray Messersmith, Ed Lucke. Hours Mon.-Fri. 8 a.m.-5 p.m., Sat. 8 a.m.-4 p.m. Customers may browse yard. Specializes in all types of vehicles from 1935-80. Approximately 400 to 500 vehicles in yard.

**Vogt's Inc.:** 2239 Old Westminster Rd., Finksburg, Md. 21048. Phone 1-800-492-1300. Jake. Hours Mon.-Fri. 8:30 a.m.-5 p.m., Sat. 8:30 a.m.-noon. Customers may browse yard. Mail-order service. Specializes in all 1935-90. Approximately 2,500 vehicles in yard. In business over 35 years.

## MASSACHUSETTS

**Arthur's Junkyard:** 147 Fremont St., Taunton, Mass. 02780. Phone 617-822-0801.

**Auto Save Yard Corp.:** Edward R. Schwartz, 800 West Roxbury Pkwy., Chestnut Hill, Mass. 02167. Phone 617-739-1900, 6 p.m.-9 p.m. SASE for reply. Mail-order service. Yard is closed but has many parts, carbs and ignition, little sheet metal. In business over 60 years.

**Curboy's Used Auto Parts:** Meshapaug Rd., Sturbridge, Mass. 01566. Phone 508-347-9650. Customers may not browse yard. Inventory of cars and parts 1960 to present.

**L & L Auto Parts:** 2091 Cedar St., Dighton, Mass. 02715. Phone 617-669-6751.

**Standard Auto Wrecking:** 257 Grant St., Worcester, Mass. 01600. Phone 617-755-8631, 755-5246 or 756-2786.

**Stevens Auto Inc.:** Joe Stevens, 162 Freeman Rd., Charlton, Mass. 01507. Phone 508-248-5539. Hours Mon.-Fri. 8 a.m.-5 p.m., Sat. 8 a.m.-2:30 p.m. Over 2,000 vehicles from the 1940s through 1980s and growing. Established and family operated since 1956.

**Ventura's Auto Parts:** 917 Somerset Ave., Taunton, Mass. 02780. Phone 617-824-9711.

**Westport Auto Salvage:** American Legion Hwy., Rt. 177, Westport, Mass. 02790. Phone 617-636-8201.

## MICHIGAN

**Bartnik Sales & Service:** 6524 Van Dyke, Cass City, Mich. 48726. Located at the corner of M-53 & M-81. Phone 517-872-3541. Jerry or Henry Bartnik. Hours Mon.-Fri. 8 a.m.-5:30 p.m., Sat. 8 a.m.-5 p.m. Customers may browse yard. Mail orders accepted. Specializes in cars and trucks from the '60s and '70s. Approximately 375 vehicles in yard. In business over 38 years.

**Bob's Auto Parts:** Bob Zimmerman, 6390 N. Lapeer Rd., Fostoria, Mich. 48435. Phone 810-793-7500. Call for hours. Approximately 2,000 antique and classic cars for parts, also new parts for old cars, ignitions, brakes, water pumps and bearings. Mail order.

**Doc's Auto Parts:** 38708 Fisk Lk. Rd., Paw Paw, Mich. 49079. Phone 616-657-5268. Walter or Mary Jane Lula. Hours Thurs.-Fri. noon-6 p.m., Sat. 8 a.m.-3 p.m. Customers may browse yard. Mail-order service available on small parts. Specializes in '30s through '70s, most makes. 600 vehicles in yard. In business over 40 years.

**Hillard's Scrapyard:** 11301 Crystal N.E., Vestaberg, Mich. 48891. Phone 517-268-5262.

**Joe's Auto Wrecking:** 14718 M 104, Spring Lake, Mich. 49456. Phone 616-842-6940. Gary Bisacky. Hours Mon.-Fri. 8 a.m.-2 p.m.

**Schultz's Auto Salvage:** 10101 N. Belsay Rd., Millington, Mich. 48746. Phone 517-871-3165. Wayne or Angela Schultz. Hours Mon.-Sat. 9 a.m.-5 p.m. Customers may browse yard. Specializes in GM products of the mid-'60s and up. Approximately 500 vehicles in yard. 24-hour wrecking service. In business over 15 years.

**Super Auto Parts:** Bernell Henderson, 6162 Lapeer Rd., Clyde, Mich. 48049. Phone 810-982-6895. Hours Mon.-Sat. 11 a.m.-5 p.m., but closed on Tues. Customers may browse yard. Handles all makes and models with majority of '50s and '60s, through most '75s all makes. Approximately 600 vehicles in yard. In business over 54 years.

## MINNESOTA

**Cedar Auto Parts:** Pat Skelley, 1100 Syndicate St., Jordan, Minn. 56011. Phone 612-492-3303, 1-800-755-3266. Hours Mon.-Fri. 8 a.m.-5:30 p.m., Sat. 8 a.m.-2 p.m. Approximately 750 cars and trucks, early and late models. Corvettes a specialty.

**Doug's Auto Parts:** Hwy. 59 North, Box 811, Marshall, Minn. 56258. Phone 507-537-1487. Doug. Hours Mon.-Fri. 8 a.m.-5 p.m. Mail-order service. Specializes in 1932-48 Fords, 1937-68 Chevys, '32-up big trucks (Fords & Chevys); have many other cars. Carries a complete line of new sheet metal and rust-repair panels. Approximately 200 vehicles in yard. In business over 19 years.

**Joe's Auto Sales:** Joe Kummer, 5849-190th St. E., Hastings, Minn. 55033. Phone 651-437-6787. Hours Mon. 9 a.m.-noon, 1 p.m.-5 p.m.; Tues.-Fri. 8 a.m.-noon, 1 p.m.-5 p.m.; Sat. 8 a.m.-1 p.m. Specializes in Ford, Mercury and Lincoln parts from 1939-89. Approximately 1,300 vehicles in yard. Sixty semi trailers full of parts. UPS service. In business since 1966.

**Mopar Mel's:** Mel Bohnenkamp, RR 2 Box 6B1, Hwy 32 North, Fertile, Minn. 56540. Phone 218-945-6920. Hours Mon.-Fri. 8 a.m.-6 p.m. Closed weekends. Visitors by appointment only. Mail-order service available. Specializing in '57-62 Mopars. Approximately 310 vehicles in yard. Services include restorations for '57-62 Mopars and parts sales for '56-66 Mopars. In business for over 26 years.

**Pine River Salvage:** Hwy. 371 North, Pine River, Minn. 56474. Phone 218-587-2700, 1-800-642-2880. Hours Mon.-Sat. 8 a.m.-6 p.m., Sun. by appointment only. Customers may browse yard. Mail-order service, SASE. Specializes in variety of makes and models 1940-80. Approximately 3,500 vehicles in yard.

**Rick's Towing, Auto Parts & Sales:** Box 92, 124 Hwy. 10, Royalton, Minn. 56373. Phone 612-584-5586, 612-654-1302, Minn. Watts 1-800-245-5588. Richard T. Kowalczyk or Jaime Hoff. Hours Mon.-Fri. 7:30 a.m.-5:30 p.m., Sat. 8 a.m.-3 p.m. Inventory list available. Customers may browse yard. Specializes in late-model domestics, cars and trucks, 4x4s. Towing available. New and used parts. Approximately 300 vehicles in yard. In business over 13 years.

**Sleepy Eye Salvage Co.:** RR 4, Box 60, Sleepy Eye, Minn. 56085. Phone 507-794-6673. Glen Jr., Gary or Glen Sr. Hours Mon.-Fri. 8:30 a.m.-6 p.m., Sat. 8:30 a.m.-4 p.m. Customers may browse yard. Mail-order service. Specializes in 1937-77 vehicles. Approximately 600 vehicles in yard. Towing available. In business over 25 years.

**Windy Hill Auto Parts:** 9200 240th Ave. NE, New London, Minn. 56273. Phone 612-354-2201. Allan, Dave, or Hannah. Hours Sun.-Sat. 7 a.m.-5 p.m. Mail-order service. Customers may browse. Specializes in American-made cars and trucks from 1915-90. Mostly older cars and trucks with nearly 8,000 cars pre-1968 and military trucks. Approximately 12,000 vehicles in yard. In business over 27 years at this location.

# MISSOURI

**Hillside Auto Salvage:** Johnny Rawlins, Rt. 4, Box 179B, Joplin, Mo. 64801. Phone 417-624-1042. Hours Tues.-Sat. 8 a.m.-dark. Customers may browse yard. Specializes in vehicles from 1941-81, including Ford products, Camaros, Corvettes, Firebirds, etc. Approximately 200 vehicles in yard. In business over four years.

**J and M Vintage Auto:** Jim or Mickie Burrowes, P.O. Box 297, Goodman, Mo. 64843. Phone 417-364-7203. Hours Tues.-Fri. 8 a.m.-5 p.m., Sat. 8 a.m.-3 p.m. Customers may browse yard. Over 1,800 cars and pickups, 1936-74.

**K.C. Thunderbird:** Don Kimrey, 5002 Gardner, Kansas City, Mo. 64120. Phone 816-241-2280. Hours 8 a.m.-11 a.m. 1958 through 1971 Thunderbirds. 240 parts cars all Thunderbirds.

**Lorenz Service:** Greg Lorenz, RR 1 Box 70, Corder, Mo. 64021. Phone 660-394-2423. Hours Mon.-Fri. 8 a.m.-6 p.m. Specializes in '30s to '70s, parts only. Approximately 600-700 vehicles in yard. In business since 1949.

**R & R Auto Salvage:** Highway 60, Aurora, Mo. Hours Mon.-Sat. 8 a.m.-5 p.m. Mailing address: Route 2, Box 196G, Verona, Mo. 65769. Phone (order line) 1-800-426-HEMI; (info line) 417-678-5551; Fax 417-678-6403.

**Trimble Farmer's Salvage, Inc.:** P.O. Box 53, Trimble, Mo. 64492. Phone 816-357-2515. V.L. Anderson. Open by appointment only Mon.-Fri. 8 a.m.-5 p.m. Mail-order service. Specializes in some old Packard parts and trim, 1956 1/2 Packard parts cars. In business over 25 years.

**Versailles Auto Salvage:** G.E. Molloy, Rt. 4, Box 255, Versailles, Mo. 65084. Phone 314-378-6278. Hours Mon.-Fri. 8 a.m.-5 p.m., Sat. 8 a.m.-noon. Customers may browse yard. Specializes in 1964 1/2 to 1973 Mustangs, Chevelles, and other older cars. Approximately 1,900 vehicles. In business over five years.

# MONTANA

**Dutton's Restorables:** 179 Ricketts Rd., Hamilton, Mont. 59840. Phone 406-363-3380. Allan Dutton, owner.

**Flathead Salvage and Storage:** Dick Lawrence, 495 Highway 82, Box 128, Somers, Mont. 59932. Phone 406-857-3791. Hours Mon.-Fri. 9 a.m.-5 p.m., Sat. call. Customers may browse yard. Mail order services. Yard specializes in vintage 1932-50 and '70s through current year. Approximately 600 vehicles in yard. Towing and storage available. In business over 9 years.

**Freman's Auto:** Neil Freman, 138 Kountz Rd., Whitehall, Mont. 59759. Phone 406-287-5436; Fax 406-287-9103. Hours Mon.-Fri. 8 a.m.-5 p.m. Parting out over 12,000 cars, 1950s, '60s and '70s, all makes and models. Sheetmetal, trim, mechanical, some project cars, restoration services available.

**Kelly's Auto Salvage:** Kelly Wolcott, 15888 Highway 93, Arlee, Mont. 59821. Phone 406-726-3400. Hours Tues.-Sat. 8 a.m.-5 p.m. Over 2,000 cars and trucks, complete chassis, lots of 1960s, '70s and '80s.

**Polson Auto Salvage:** 54826 Highway 93, Polson, Mont. 59860. Telephone 406-883-6860. Duane Olsen.

**Marshall Sanders:** Box 1195 Shalkaho Hwy., Hamilton, Mont. 59840. Phone 406-363-328.

**Timberlane Auto:** 41 Timberlane Rd., Ronan, Mont. 59864. Phone 406-676-8111, 406-676-8112. Hours 9 a.m.-5 p.m., closed Sun.

**Wisher's Auto Recycling:** 2190 Airport Rd., Kallispell, Mont. 59901. Phone 406-752-2461. Clem or Jerry Wisher. Hours Mon.-Fri. 8:30 a.m.-5:30 p.m., Sat. 8:30 a.m.-1 p.m. Inventory list available. Specializes in all makes from 1950-88. Approximately 1,200 vehicles in yard. Towing, Mll satellite systems hot line. Offers frame work, mechanical, body and paint services. In business over 30 years.

**Young's Enterprises:** Dennis Young, 2870 Highway 2 West, Kalispell, Mont. 59901. Phone 406-755-6043. Hours 9 a.m.-5 p.m., Sat. by appointment, closed Sun. 50-70 Chevrolets. 348 & 409 cars & parts.

**Zimp's Enterprises:** 2800 So. Montana, Butte, Mont. 59701. Phone 406-782-5674. Ed or Yvonne Zimpel. Hours Mon.-Sat. 8 a.m.-6 p.m. Inventory list available. Customers may browse yard. Specializes in antiques. Approximately 60 antique vehicles for parts and 100 later models from 1950-79. In business over 10 years.

# NEBRASKA

**Eastern Nebraska Auto Recyclers:** Mile Marker 351 on Hwy. 34, P.O. Box 266, Elmwood, Neb. 68349. Phone 402-994-4555, 402-475-1135. Dan Buckner or Roger Pickering. Hours Mon.-Fri. 9 a.m.-6 p.m., Sat. 9 a.m.-4 p.m. Customers may browse yard. Mail-order service. Specializes in postwar cars, late '40s through '80s. Has restorable complete cars and parts cars. Approximately 1,500 vehicles in yard. Offers towing and repair work. In business over 15 years.

**W.L. 'Wally' Mansfield:** 214 N. 13th St., Wymore, Neb. 68466-1640. Phone 402-645-3546. Hours by appointment only. Pre-war cars and trucks and parts. Specializes in Ford, Chevy, Dodge, Nash and Buick. Lots of windshields, rims, radiators and motors. Collecting since 1944.

**Osintowski's Repair:** RR 1, Box 107, Genoa, Neb. 68640. Phone 402-678-2650. Pat Osintowski. Hours Mon.-Sat. 8 a.m.-8 p.m. Customers may browse yard. Specializing in Mopar and Chrysler cars & parts '50-70s, Pontiacs from '60s & '70s. Assorted cars from '60s. Approximately 250 cars in yard. Hauling service offered. In business over nine years.

**Sullivan Salvage & Recycling:** Gil Sullivan, Hemingford, Neb. 69348. Phone 308-487-

3755. Approximately 100-150 cars in yard.

# NEVADA

**All Auto Inc or Mustang Auto Wrecking:** Rural Route 1, Mustang, Sparks, Nev. 89431. Phone 702-342-0225. Hours Mon.-Fri. 9 a.m.-5 p.m., Sat. 9 a.m.-1 p.m.

**K & L Auto Wrecking:** 4540 Hammer Lane, Las Vegas, Nev. 89115. Phone 702-644-5544.

**Ken's Auto Wrecking:** Ken Phillips, 5051 Coppersage St., Las Vegas, Nev. 89115. Phone 702-643-1516. Hours Mon.-Fri. 10 a.m.-4 p.m., Sat. 10 a.m.-1 p.m. Customers may browse yard. Mail-order service. Specializes in AMCs from 1953-80, T-Birds from 1958-78, Chrysler products from 1956-80. Approximately 360 vehicles in yard. Custom motor rebuilds for restorations. In business over 14 years.

**Larry's Auto Wrecking:** Larry M. Whittaker, 4160 Studio St., Las Vegas, Nev. 89115. Phone 702-644-1671. Hours Mon.-Fri. 8 a.m.-5 p.m., Sat. 8 a.m.-12 noon. Shipping available throughout the U.S. Approximately 600 vehicles in yard.

**Murray's Salvage Co.:** Dick Murray, 6051 N. Hollywood, Las Vegas, Nev. 89115. Phone 702-644-3324. Open normal business hours seven days a week. Antique, classic and special interest parts and accessories. Recycles hundreds of cars and trucks every year.

**S & M Vintage Auto:** 2560 Solari Dr., Reno, Nev. 89509. Phone 702-826-0257. Mike or Sandy Tackett. Open by appointment. Customers may browse yard. Mail-order service. Specializes in Ford Products, mid '50s to early '70s. Approximately 150 vehicles in yard. Offers mechanical parts, both new and used. Towing anywhere. In business since 1983.

**Southwest Auto Wrecking:** Robert Dippner, 4515 E. Smiley Rd., Las Vegas, Nev. 89115. Phone 702-643-1771. Hours Mon.-Fri. 8 a.m.-4:30 p.m., Sat. 8 a.m.-2:30 p.m. Customer may browse yard. Approximately 4,500 vehicles in yard. Older American rust free-sheet metal. Offers auto glass, new aftermarket sheet metal, and accessories. In business over 12 years.

# NEW HAMPSHIRE

**Lane's Garage & Auto Body:** RFD 8, Box 365, Loudon, N.H. 03301. On Rt. 106, 10 miles north of Concord. Phone 603-783-4752. Hours Mon.-Fri. 8 a.m.-6 p.m., weekends by appointment only. Handles all makes and models of 1930s through late '60s. Has restorable cars and parts cars.

# NEW JERSEY

**Studebaker Sanctuary:** Ralph Banghart, 425 Washburn Ave., Washington, N.J. 07882. Phone 908-689-3509. Hours by appointment only. High quality antique auto repair specializing in Studebakers.

NOS and used Studebaker parts, also Studebaker cars and trucks for sale. Also engine swaps, custom fabrication, mig-arc & gas welding; exhaust bending, also other miscellaneous autos for sale.

## NEW MEXICO

Discount Auto Parts: 4703 Broadway S.E., Albuquerque, N.M. 87105. Phone 505-877-6782. Hours Mon.-Fri. 8 a.m.-5:30 p.m., Sat. 8 a.m.-1 p.m. Customers may browse yard supervised. Specializes in new and used VW parts day one through 1985. Approximately 1,400 vehicles in yard.

## NEW YORK

Adler's Antique Autos, Inc.: Bob Adler, 801 NY Route 43, Stephentown, N.Y. 12168. Phone 518-733-5749; advdesign1 @aol.com. Hours Mon.-Fri. 9 a.m.-5 p.m. Mail order. Specializes in Chevrolet 1930-80 cars, 1947-55 trucks. Approximately 650 vehicles in yard. Complete restoration facility and Chevrolet research library. In business over 26 years.

Bob & Art's Auto Parts: 2641 Reno Rd., Schodack Center, Castleton, N.Y. 12033. Phone 518-477-9183. Bob Jeannin or Art Carkner. Hours Mon.-Sun. 1-5 p.m. Customers may browse yard by special arrangement only. Mail-order service. Specializes in late '40s to late '60s, AMCs to '80s (especially Ramblers), many Hudsons, also Studebakers, Fords, GM models and Mopars. Approximately 1,000 vehicles in yard. In business since 1958.

British Auto: Mark Voelckers, 600 Penfield Rd., Macedon, N.Y. 14502. Phone 315-986-3097. Hours Mon.-Fri. 8 a.m.-5 p.m. Specializes in English cars only, 1950 to present. Approximately 700 cars, parts from another 400. Complete expert repair service. Importer. Information source and parts locator. Large inventory of new, used and NOS. In business over 19 years.

Mountain Fuel: Russell Van Aken, RFD #2, Hubbard Rd., Gilboa, N.Y. 12076. Open dawn to dusk weekends only. 50 year collection. Specializing in cars, machinery and parts for restoring. Over 200.

Nash Auto Parts: Joseph Nash, Pump Rd., Weedsport, N.Y. 13166. Phone 315-252-5878, 1-800-526-6334. Hours Mon.-Fri. 9 a.m.-5 p.m., Sat. 9 a.m.-1 p.m. Customers may browse yard. Mail orders and phone orders accepted. Handles all makes 1920-1990, NOS, used and NORS parts available. Firm offers teletype locating of parts, bead blasting and cleaning to over 1,500 other salvage yards. Approximately 3,000 vehicles in yard. In business since 1952.

Red Praetorius: 1935 Rt. 32, Saugerties, N.Y. 12477. Phone 914-246-9930. Open by appointment only. Customers may browse yard. Will sell whole parts cars, 1920-1960 available. Approximately 1,000 vehicles in yard. In business over 35 years.

Saw Mill Auto Wreckers: 12 Worth St., Yonkers, N.Y. 10701. Located two blocks off North Lockwood Ave. Phone 914-968-5300.

Sil's Foreign Auto Parts, Inc.: 1498 Spur Dr. So., Islip, N.Y. 11751. Phone 516-581-7624. Yulands Dilovc. Hours Mon.-Fri. 8 a.m.-4:30 p.m., Sat. 9 a.m.-3 p.m. Mail orders accepted. Specializes in late-model European and Japanese cars.

Tucker's Auto Salvage: Richard J. Tucker, RD, Box 170, Burke, N.Y. 12917. Phone 518-483-5478. Hours Mon.-Fri. 8 a.m.-5 p.m., Sat. 8 a.m.-noon. Mail orders accepted. Customers may browse yard. Approximately 1,000 vehicles in yard. Firm has several parts cars from the postwar era, Studebaker cars and trucks. NOS and used parts available. Mechanical repairs, body work and sandblasting services available. In business over 20 years.

## NORTH CAROLINA

Thunderbird Barn: 2919 Elkin Hwy 268, North Wilkesboro, N.C. 28659. Phone 910-667-0837. Don Hayes. Hours Mon.-Fri. 9 a.m.-5 p.m., Sat. 9 a.m.-noon. Customers may browse yard. Mail-order service. Specializes in 1958 through 1969 T-Birds. Approximately 50 vehicles in yard. In business over 11 years.

## NORTH DAKOTA

East End Auto Parts: 75-10th Ave. E, Box 183, Dickinson, N.D. 58601. Phone 701-225-4206. Hours Mon.-Friday 8 a.m.-5 p.m., Sat. 8 a.m.- noon. Inventory list is available. Customers may browse yard. Mail-order service. Specializes in '40s, '50s, '60s, '70s and '80s Chevys, Fords, Dodges and foreign. Over 1,200 vehicles in yard. Towing services. In business over 30 years.

Porter Auto Iron & Metal: Kenneth Porter, Rt. 1, Box 180, Park River, N.D. 58270. Phone 701-284-6517. Hours Mon.-Fri. 8 a.m.-5 p.m., Sat. 8 a.m.-noon. Specializes in buying aluminum cans, all kinds of metals. Older vehicles in yard. Offers welding. In business over 27 years.

Walker's Garage: Leroy Walker, HC 3, Box 38, Beulah, N.D. 58523. Hours Mon.-Fri. 8:30 a.m.-5 p.m., Sat. 8:30 a.m.-3 p.m. Phone 701-873-4489. Escorted browsing permitted. Approximately 3500 parts cars, with 198 Edsels.

## OHIO

American Parts Depot: Doug Noel, 409 N. Main St, West Manchester, Ohio 45382. Phone 513-678-7249. Hours Mon.-Fri. 8 a.m.-12 noon, 1 p.m.-6 p.m.; Wed. evens. 7 p.m.-10 p.m. Located on several acres to the west side of Route 127, 6 miles north of I-70, 10 miles east of the Indiana line.

Arlington Auto Wrecking: 445 North Arlington St., Akron, Ohio 44305-1687. Phone 216-434-3466. Hours Mon.-Fri. 8 a.m.-5 p.m., Sat. 8 a.m.-4 p.m. Customers may browse yard. Mail-order service. Specializes in standard transmissions, plus many hard to find driveline parts. Approximately 500 vehicles in yard. Over 51 years in the recycling business.

Bob's Auto Wrecking: 12602 Rt. 13, Milan, Ohio 44846. Phone 419-499-2415. North off Rt. 250 1/2 mile south of Ohio turnpike. Bob or Mark Reer. Hours Mon.-Fri. 8 a.m.-5 p.m., Sat. 8 a.m.-noon. Specializes in all makes from 1950-93 cars & small trucks. Approximately 5,000 in yard. In business over 32 years.

Cherry Auto Parts: 5650 N. Detroit Ave., Toledo, Ohio 43612. Phone 419-476-7222, 1-800-537-8677. Mark and Nevin Liber. Hours Mon.-Fri. 7 a.m.-5 p.m., Sat. 8:30 a.m.-noon. Mail-order service available. Specializes in Asian cars and trucks '85-91 and European cars '80-91. Full machine shop. Approximately 800 vehicles in yard. In business over 44 years.

Del-Car Auto Parts: 5501 Westerville, P.O. Box 157, 5501 Westerville Rd., Westerville, Ohio 43081. Phone 614-882-0220; Fax 614-895-1399. John or Ken Parrish. Hours Mon.-Fri. 8 a.m.-5 p.m. Mail-order service. Specializes in American cars and trucks, 1983 to current. Approximately 1,300 vehicles in yard. Offers towing services. In business over 22 years.

Del-Car Auto Wrecking: 6650 Harlem Rd., Westerville, Ohio 43081. Phone 614-882-0777; Fax 614-895-1399. John or Ken Parrish. Hours Mon.-Fri. 8 a.m.-5 p.m. Mail order services. Specializes in American cars and trucks from 1965-92. In business over 22 years.

File's Auto Wrecking: Paul File, 936 Scoville-North Rd., Vienna, Ohio 44473. Phone 330-539-5114. Hours Mon.-Sat. 9 a.m.-5 p.m., Sun. 9 a.m.-3 p.m. 1950-80s, many Cadillac, Lincoln, foreign vehicles. Major credit cards. Located near Warren-Youngstown area.

Graveyard Auto Parts: Joseph R. Downey, 3383 Kuhn Rd., Coldwater, Ohio 45828. Phone 419-586-1367. Normal business hours. More than 1,900 vehicles. Parts for late model and vintage cars and trucks. Huge collection of old Packards, ranging from the late '40s to 1956. Customers may browse yard. In business since 1972.

Ron's Auto Parts: 3590 Center Rd., Zanesville, Ohio 43701. Phone 614-453-7234. Ron or Kathy Hall. Hours Mon.-Fri. 8 a.m.-5 p.m., Sat. 8 a.m.-2 p.m. Customers may browse yard. Specializes in all makes from early '40s to present. Approximately 3,000 vehicles in yard. In business over 25 years.

Schulte Auto Wrecking: John Schulte, 3737 Logan-Gate, Youngstown, Ohio 44505. Phone 330-759-9500. Hours 9 a.m.-5 p.m. daily. 1940's to 1980's.

Stark Wrecking Co.: 7081 Germantown Pike, Miamisburg, Ohio 45342. Phone 513-866-5032. Clarence Witte. Hours Mon.-Sat. 9 a.m.-5 p.m. No mail order. Self-service, pull your own parts. About 3,000 cars from '20s-80s. In business at the same location for over 70 years.

Twilight Taxi Parts, Inc.: Ben Merkel, 14503 Old State Rd. Rt. 608, Middlefield, Ohio 44062. Phone 216-632-5419, noon-4 p.m. Hours Mon.-Fri. 9 a.m.-4 p.m. By appointment only on weekends. Customers may browse yard. Specializes in Checker motors products, mostly 1960-82. Approximately 160 vehicles in yard. In business over three years.

## OKLAHOMA

**Aabar's Cadillac & Lincoln Salvage:** Bruce Duckworth, 9700 N.E. 23rd, Oklahoma City, Okla. 73141. Phone 405-769-3318; Fax 405-769-9542. Hours Mon.-Fri. 9 a.m.-5:30 p.m. We are worldwide suppliers of used, NORS and NOS parts for Cadillacs and Lincolns. Solid used sheetmetal, bumpers, grilles, chrome, taillights, etc. Ship anywhere, all major credit cards.

**Classic Auto Parts:** 2040 N. Yale, Tulsa, Okla. 74115.

**Country Auto:** Melba Holik, Rt. 4, Box 125A, Chandler, Okla. 74834. Phone 405-258-0957 or 405-567-3105; www.expage.com/page/countryauto. Hours vary, call for appointment. Complete cars to be restored. Most are 1950-60s. Handle Fords, Mopars, Studebakers, Packards, Mercedes, Opels, Fiats and GM.

**Hauf Antique & Classic Cars:** Gene and Jo Hauf, P.O. Box 547, Stillwater, Okla. 74076. Phone 405-372-1585; Fax 405-372-1586. Hours Tues.-Fri. 8 a.m.-5:30 p.m., Sun. by appointment only. 1930-89 cars and pickups. We ship UPS, bus, mail or truck line. In business over 48 years.

**Joe Ersland Antique Cars:** Joe and Sandy Ersland, P.O. Box 562, Chickasha, Okla. 73023-0562. Phone 405-224-2049, 405-222-3047 or 405-779-7108. Call ahead. A collection of cars, auto memorabilia and an assortment of heavy old trucks which date back into the early teens and '50s. Approximately 100 vehicles for sale.

**Johnson's Wrecker Service:** Bill Johnson, 3602 So. Hwy. 81, Chickasha, Okla. 73018. Phone 405-224-2800. Hours Mon.-Fri. 9:30 a.m.-5:30 p.m. Please phone ahead. Towing of heavy to light vehicles. Only complete vehicles are sold.

**North Yale Auto Parts, Inc.:** Rt. 1, Box 707, Sperry, Okla. 74073. Phone 918-288-7218, 1-800-256-6927; Fax 918-288-7223. Walt or Bobby Ward. Hours Mon.-Fri. 8 a.m.-5 p.m., Sat. 9 a.m.-noon. Ford, Chrysler, GM. 50 to 80 vehicles. Rust free auto parts. UPS, truck.

**31 Auto Salvage:** Rt. 5, McAlester, Okla. 74501. Phone 918-423-2022. Hours Mon.-Fri. 8 a.m.-5 p.m., Sat. 8 a.m.-noon. Customers may browse yard. Mail-order service. Specializes in 1960-72 General Motors. Approximately 250 vehicles in yard. In business over 15 years.

## OREGON

**Brad's Auto & Truck Parts:** Lisa Stroup, 2618 S. Highway 97, Redmond, Ore. 97756. Phone 541-923-2723; Fax 541-923-3113. Hours Mon.-Fri. 8 a.m.-5 p.m., Sat. 10 a.m.-2 p.m.

**D & R Auto Sales:** David Spangenberg, Rt. 2 Box 2080, Hermiston, Ore. 97838. Phone 541-567-8048, (outside OR) 1-800-554-

8763. Hours Mon.-Fri. 9:30 a.m.-6:30 p.m., Sat. 10:30 a.m.-6 p.m. Inventory list available. Customers may browse yard. Yard specializes in all makes and models, preferably pre-1970 vehicles through 1926. Selling whole vehicles, not parting out. Approximately 500 vehicles in yard. Offers towing, delivery, restoration, and location of special interest autos.

**Faspec British Cars & Parts:** 1036 SE Stark St., Portland, Ore. 97214. Phone 1-800-547-8788 (outside OR), 541-232-1232 (OR). Larry Mosen. Hours Mon.-Fri 9 a.m.-6 p.m., Sat. 9 a.m.-12:30 p.m. Mail orders accepted. Specializes in new and used parts. Catalogs available for all models of MG, Austin-Healey, Triumph or Spridget. Approximately 100 vehicles in yard. Firm also sells British used cars. In business over 24 years.

**Ira's Sales and Service:** 181 S.W. Merritt Lane, Madras, Ore. 97741. Phone 541-475-3861. Ira Merritt, owner. Hours Mon.-Fri. 8 a.m.-5 p.m.

**Klamath Auto Wreckers:** 3315 Washburn Way, Klamath Falls, Ore. 97603. Phone 541-882-1677; 1-800-452-3301 (OR, NV, CA only). Hours Mon.-Fri. 8 a.m.-5 p.m., Sat. 9 a.m.-1 p.m.

**McCoy's Auto and Truck Wrecking:** 32989 Lynx Hollow Rd., Creswell, Ore. 97426. Phone 541-942-0804. Hours Mon.-Fri. 8:30 a.m.-5:30 p.m., Sat. 8:30 a.m.-3 p.m. Mail order services. Inventory list available. Customers may browse yard. Yard specializes in all makes and model, 1950-85. Approximately 700 vehicles in yard. In business over 11 years.

**George Merricks:** George Merrick, Bend, Ore. Phone 541-382-6134. Open by appointment only, call from 8 a.m.-8 p.m.

**Old Car Parts:** Gary Novak, 7525 SE Powell, Portland, Ore. 97206. Phone 503-771-9416. By appointment only. Chevy haven.

**Rainbow Auto Wreckers:** 25850 Tidball Lane, Veneta, Ore. 97487. Phone 541-935-1828, 1-800-303-1828. Leo and Emma Hecht. Hours Mon.-Sat. 8:30 a.m.-5 p.m. Specializing in 1955-64 Chevy cars and pickup parts, also other makes, models and years.

**Route 97 Trading Post:** Brad & Sharon Carrell. Phone 541-389-6079.

## PENNSYLVANIA

**Eperthener's Auto Wrecking:** Ron Eperthener Jr., 683 Tieline Rd., Grove City, Pa. 16127. Hours Mon.-Fri. 9 a.m.-5 p.m., Sat. 9 a.m.-noon. Phone 814-786-7173. Browsing by request. All parts removed by staff. In business since 1957.

**Feezle's Auto Wrecking:** Jim and Rick Feezle, RD 1, Box 215, Enon Valley, Pa. 16120. Phone 412-336-5755, 412-336-5512. Hours Mon.-Fri. 8:30 a.m.-5 p.m., Sat. 8:30 a.m.-4 p.m. Approximately 1,200 pickups, 2,500 cars and 2,000 motorcycles. Many late '50s and early '60s models. In business since 1979.

**The Junkyard:** 201 Cedar St., Allentown, Pa. 18102. Phone 215-435-7278. Hours Mon.-Fri. 9 a.m.-6 p.m., Sat. 9 a.m.-4 p.m. Customers may browse yard. Specializes in all makes 1980 and older. Over 1,000 vehicles in yard. In business over 4 years.

**Klinger's Used Auto Sales:** Dean H. Klinger, RD 3, Box 454, Pine Grove, Pa. 17963. Phone 717-345-8778. Hours Mon.-Fri. 9 a.m.-5 p.m., Sat. 8 a.m.-4 p.m., closed Sun. Inventory list available. Customers may browse yard. Many cars from 1941-54 (Chevy), later models 1963-83. Most makes and models. Approximately 2,500 vehicles in yard. In business over 14 years.

**Ed Lucke's Auto Parts:** RR 2, Box 2883, Glenville, Pa. 17329. Phone 717-235-2866. C. Edwin Lucke. Hours Mon.-Fri. 9 a.m.-5 p.m., Sat. 9 a.m.-noon. Parts for domestic vehicles 1935-85. Have several thousand vehicles and many parts removed.

**Charlie Reinert's Garage:** Charlie Reinert, corner of Farmington Ave. and East St., Pottstown, Pa. Phone 610-326-1084. Four cars, nine vans and several trailer-loads of parts. Most parts are for Corvairs. Willing to sell the inventory piece-by-piece if necessary.

**Secco Auto Parts:** Box 271-B, Hayes Rd., Kersey, Pa. 15846. Phone 814-885-6370. Leroy Secco. Open by appointment only. Customers may browse yard. Mail orders accepted. Yard specializes in makes from the '50s, '60s and early '70s, also parts for 1941-49 and 1953 Ford flathead engines. Interested in selling out. Approximately 1,000 vehicles in yard. In business over 30 years.

**Winnick's Auto Sales & Parts:** Rt. 61, P.O. Box 476, Shamokin, Pa. 17872. Phone 717-648-6857. Located on Rt. 61 between Shamokin & Kulpmont. Hours Mon.-Fri. 8 a.m.-5 p.m., Sat. 8 a.m.-noon. Inventory list available. Customers may browse yard. Mail-order service. Specializes in '65 to '75 Mustangs and Camaro cars & all old make vehicles. Parts for American & imported cars and trucks. Approximately 500 vehicles in yard. In business over 50 years.

## RHODE ISLAND

**Arnold's Auto Parts:** 1484 Crandall Rd., Tiverton, R.I. 02878. Phone 401-624-6936. Doug Waite. Hours Mon.-Fri. 8 a.m.-5 p.m., Sat. 8 a.m.-3 p.m. Customers may browse yard. Mail-order service. Specializes in American cars and trucks from '30s to '70s. Approximately 1,000 vehicles in yard. Towing, referrals. In business since 1952.

**Bill's Auto Parts:** 1 Macondry St., Cumberland, R.I. 02864. Phone 401-725-1225. Hours Mon.-Fri. 8 a.m.-4:30 p.m., Sat. 8 a.m.-4 p.m., Sun. 9 a.m.-3 p.m. Inventory list is available. Customers may browse yard. Yard specializes in foreign and domestic, mostly '70s and early '80s with some '50-60s. Approximately 1,000 vehicles in yard. New parts can be ordered. In business over 30 years.

**Wilson's Auto Parts:** Mill Rd., Foster, R.I. 02825. Phone 401-647-3400.

## SOUTH CAROLINA

**Clinkscales Garage & Recycling:** Sonny Clinkscales, 2433 Hwy. 252, Belton, S.C. 29627. Phone 864-338-6944. Hours are Mon.-Fri. 8 a.m.-5:30 p.m., Sat. by appointments only. Approximately 550 to 600 cars from the '50s and '60s, some date back to the '30s. In business since 1957.

**Cook's Garage:** J.P. Cook, 201 Callison Hwy., Greenwood, S.C. 29646. Phone 864-227-2731. Hours Mon.-Fri. 8 a.m.-6 p.m. Mail orders accepted. Used cars, new and used parts, auto restorations.

**Marshall Royston:** 316 Hwy 221 S, Greenwood, S.C. 29646. Phone 803-227-2598. Cars in the yard range from '40s to late '60s. Approximately 200 vehicles in the yard. In business over 30 years.

## SOUTH DAKOTA

**Howard's Corvettes:** Howard Goehring, RR 3, Box 162, Sioux Falls, S.D. 57106. Phone 605-368-5233. Hours Mon.-Fri. 9 a.m.-5:30 p.m., Sat. 9 a.m.-4 p.m. Inventory list available. Mail-order service. Specializes in 1968-88 Corvettes. Approximately 40 vehicles in yard. In business over 19 years.

**Jim's Auto Salvage:** Jim or Cyndi Dempsey, HCR 75, Box 4, Sturgis, S.D. 57785. Phone 605-347-2303; Fax 605-347-5636. Hours Mon.-Fri. 8 a.m.-5:30 p.m. Many project cars, from 1940s to 1970s. Parts and complete cars.

**Wayne's Auto Salvage:** Wayne Myers, RR 3, Box 41, Winner, S.D. 57580. Phone 605-842-2054. Hours Mon.-Fri. 9 a.m.-6 p.m., Sat. 10 a.m.-4 p.m. Customers may browse yard. Mail-order service. Specializes in 1937-70 Fords, Chevys, Plymouths, Dodges, etc., 1946-48 Ford coupes, plus Hudsons, Studebakers, Kaisers, Frazers, Nashes, etc. Approximately 1,500 vehicles in yard. Offers mechanical and muffler shop. In business over 26 years.

**Ziegler King Salvage:** 41946 287th St., Tripp, S.D. 57376. Open by appointment only. Used cars, trucks, farm tractors and machinery of pre-'62 vintage. Sells complete vehicles or parts. Approximately 2,000 cars in yard.

## TENNESSEE

**Cars and Parts:** Ernest Lumpkin, Rt. 1, Dyer, Tenn. 38330. Phone 901-643-6448. Hours Mon.-Sat. 6 a.m.-8 p.m. Customers may browse yard. Mail-order service. Specializes in Model A and T Fords, early V-8 Fords, some dating back to the '30s. Four barns full of parts. Over 30 vehicles in yard. In business over 20 years.

**Corvair Ranch, Inc.:** 1079 Bon-Air Rd., Gettysburg, Pa. 17325. Phone 717-624-2805. Hours Mon.-Sat. 8 a.m.-6 p.m. Handles only Corvairs. Offers NOS, used and reproduction parts. Auto sales, repairs and restoration. Parts shipping is available. Customers can browse the yard.

**Holt's Auto Salvage:** Claude Holt, Hwy 431, Fayetteville, Tenn. Phone 615-433-2501, 615-433-2900. Call before visiting. Approximately 3,000 vehicles in yard. In business over 33 years.

**Lane Auto Salvage:** Highway 127, Jamestown, Tenn. 38556. No phone calls. No mail-order business. J.C. Lane for appointment to visit.

**LaMance Autoworks:** P.A. LaMance, P.O. Box 914, 914 Old Mill Rd., Wartburg, Tenn. 37887. Phone 423-346-7350. Customers may browse yard by appointment only. Mail-order service. Specializes in domestic cars, mid-'60s and older. Collecting auto related toys from '50s and '60s. Specializing in the toy truck "Johnny Express" from 1965. Approximately 175 vehicles in yard. In business over 18 years.

**Gale Smyth Antique Auto:** 8316 East A.J. Hwy., Whitesburg, Tenn. 37891. Phone 615-235-5221. Hours Mon.-Sat. 8 a.m.-6 p.m. Inventory list available. Customers may browse yard. Mail-order service. Specializes in 1935 to 1972 American makes. Approximately 1,300 vehicles in yard. Offers re-chromed bumpers. In business over 20 years.

**Sonny's Auto Parts:** P.O. Box 252, Highway 11W, Blaine, Tenn. 37709. Phone 615-932-2610, 615-933-9137. Mike or Gary Reeser. Hours Mon.-Sat. 9 a.m.-5 p.m. Customers may browse yard. Cars from the '30s to '60s. Approximately 3,000 vehicles in yard.

**Volunteer State Chevy Parts:** P.O. Drawer D, Greenbrier, Tenn. 37073. Phone 615-643-4583. Paul or Don. Open by appointment only, Mon.-Fri. 8 a.m.-5:30 p.m., weekends, holidays. Call before visiting. Specializing in early '50s-'70s Chevy cars and trucks, few '40s. Less than 100 Chevys, no Corvairs, no Corvettes.

**Waldron Auto Salvage:** 5356 Murfreesboro Rd., La Vergne, Tenn. 37086. Phone 615-793-2791. Hours Mon.-Fri. 8 a.m.-5 p.m., Sat. 8 a.m.-noon. Customers may browse yard supervised. Specializes in 1960 to 1975 American cars and pickup trucks. Approximately 1,200 vehicles in yard. In business over 38 years.

## TEXAS

**Action Auto Recyclers:** Charles Pehl, P.O. Box 352, 2421 E. Hwy. 36, Temple, Tex. 76503. Phone 254-773-6201; Fax 254-742-0395; www:traderonline.com/d/actionautos. Hours Mon.-Fri. 8 a.m.-5:30 p.m., Sat. 8 a.m.-12 noon. Approximately 350 Mustangs all years. Over 200 1940-72 vehicles. Shipping available.

**Chevy Craft:** Wm. R. Clement, 3414 Quirt, Lubbock, Tex. 79404. Phone 806-747-4848; Fax 806-747-9037. Hours Mon.-Fri. 9 a.m.-6 p.m. by appointment only. Catalog is available. Tours of yard charge. Mail-order service. Specializes in V-8 fully framed Chevrolets 1955-63, 1964-72 Chevelles, Corvettes to 1971, factory power packs and 409 models. No trucks or Novas. Approximately 400 vehicles in yard. Offers show-quality chrome plating. In business over 27 years.

**CTC Auto Ranch:** David, Allen and Dale Williamson, 3077 Memory Lane, Sanger, Tex. 76266-7329. Phone 940-482-3007, 1-800-482-6199, Fax 940-482-3010. Hours Mon.-Fri. 8:30 a.m.-5:30 p.m., Sat. 9 a.m.-1 p.m. Approximately 2,600 cars. Most cars date to the '50s and '60s. Customers are not allowed to pull parts. In business since 1985.

**Henderson Auto Parts:** Edmond Dwight Baker, P.O. Box 54, Seagoville, Tex. 75159. Phone 214-287-4787. Hours Mon.-Sat. 8 a.m.-6 p.m. Inventory list available. Customers may browse yard. Specializes in all makes of 1976 and earlier. Approximately 750 vehicles in yard. In business over 15 years.

**Honest John's Caddy Corner:** John Foust, 2271 FM 407 West, P.O. Box 741, Justin, Tex. 76247. Phone 888-592-2339, 940-648-3330; Fax 940-648-9135. Hours Mon.-Fri. 9 a.m.-6 p.m. Mail-order service. Specializing in all Cadillacs 1936-80. Approximately 300 vehicles. Offering restoration, service, NOS parts, and reproduction parts. In business over eight years. www.honestjohn.com.

**Snyder Bros. Garage & Auto Wrecking:** Gene, Frank & Alan Snyder, Rt. 4, Box 25, Whitney, Tex. 76692. Phone 254-582-9746. Hours Mon.-Fri. 8 a.m.-5 p.m., Sat. 8 a.m.-noon. Approximately 300 cars, among them are around 50 Nashes. All parts are pulled for the customer. In present location since 1970.

**Texas Acres:** Ron Stitt, 1130 East FM 2410, Harker Heights, Tex. 76548. Phone 800-667-2764; Fax 254-698-4393. Hours Mon.-Fri. 9 a.m.-5 p.m. Sat. by appointment only. One of Texas largest ABCEF body only suppliers. Thousands of parts inventoried. We sell only Chrysler products. UPS & truck freight daily.

**"Texas Exports" Little Valley Auto Ranch:** Danny and Mike Barkley, Rt. 7, Box 7085, Belton, Tex. 76513. Phone 254-939-8548, cell phone 254-760-7431. Hours Mon.-Fri. 9:30 a.m.-5:30 p.m., Sat. 9:30 a.m.-4 p.m. More than 600 vintage cars, including some 75 Chevys from 1955-57. Thousands of rare parts. Delivery of parts and complete cars is available. In business since 1981.

## VIRGINIA

**Auto Krafters, Inc.:** Ron Miller, 522 S. Main St., Box 8, Broadway, Va. 22815. Phone 540-896-5910; Fax 540-896-6412; akraft@shentel.net; autokrafters.com. Hours Mon.-Fri. 8:30 a.m.-6 p.m.; Sat. 9 a.m.-12 noon. Currently parting out Fords of late '50s thru '70s. Specializing in Fairlanes, Torinos and Broncos. New parts arriving daily. 1-800-478-853.

**Glade Mountain Antique and Used Auto Parts:** Luther J. Henderlite, 6711 Lee Highway, Atkins, Va. 24311. Phone 540-783-5678. Take exit off I-81, west 1 mile on U.S. 11, south 1 mile on Va. 708, east on Va. 615, new exit 54. Hours 1 p.m.-8 p.m. Sun. May-Aug. Special hours by appointment.

Over 200 parts cars 1935-65.

**Leon's Auto Parts:** Leon Thompson, Jr., Hwy. 29, Leon, Va. 22725. Phone 540-547-2366. Hours Mon.-Fri. 8 a.m.-4 p.m., Sat. 8 a.m.-12 p.m. 10,000 '50s and '60s cars, some back to the '20s and in to the '80s. In business since 1962.

**Philbates Auto Wrecking, Inc.:** George A. Philbates, Hwy 249, P.O. Box 28, New Kent, Va. 23124. Phone 804-843-9787. Hours Mon.-Fri. 9 a.m.-5 p.m., Sat. 9 a.m.-2 p.m. Mail-order service. Customers may browse yard. Specializes in makes from 1940-78. Parts locating service for hard to find parts. Approximately 6,000 vehicles in yard. Towing services. In business over 37 years.

**Ralph's Auto Salvage and Repair:** Ralph Frank, Route 1, Box 322, Linville, Va. Phone 703-833-6111. Hours Mon.-Fri. 8 a.m.-6 p.m., closed Sat.-Sun. Approximately 200 vehicles on 10 acres. Several makes represented with majority in Fords and Chevrolets ranging from the '30s to the 70s. Sells whole cars and parts. Visitors may browse. In business since 1941.

## WASHINGTON

**A-1 Auto Wrecking:** 13818 Pacific Ave., Tacoma, Wash. 98444. Phone 206-537-3445. Hours 10 a.m.-5 p.m., Mon.-Sat. Standard transmission parts, new & used. We part out older American cars '50s, '60s, '70s Mopar, GM and Ford. In business since 1948 at same location.

**Antique Auto Items:** S. 1607 McCabe Rd., Spokane, Wash. 99216. Phone 509-926-0987. Darrell or Donna Rosenkranz. Open by appointment only. Send specific list of items needed with SASE. Small items from closed yard. Mail-order small parts for over 30 years.

**Antique Auto Ranch:** N. 2225 Dollar Rd., Spokane, Wash. 99212. Phone 509-535-7789. Tom or Gary. Hours Mon.-Fri. 8 a.m.-5 p.m., Sat. 8 a.m.-2 p.m. Customers may browse yard. Mail-order service. Specializes in American makes, 1962 and older. Large inventory of new old stock (NOS). Over 200 vehicles in yard. Offers chassis restoration including all sub components. In business over 33 years.

**Dan's Garage:** Daniel F. Stafford, 508 E. Bruneau Ave., Kennewick, Wash. 99336. Phone 509-586-2579. General Motors only. Autowrecking. Approximately 500 cars, late 1950s to '70s. Specializing in Chevy and Pontiac. We ship UPS or truck.

**DBaer's Cadillac Ville:** Don Baer, P.O. Box B, Winlock, Wash. 98596. Phone 360-785-4133; Fax 360-269-0498. Hours Mon.-Fri. 10 a.m.-6 p.m. Warehouse plus more than 1,000 retired Cadillacs. 1949-85. Mail order only. Visa, MC, AMX, M/O, COD.

**Ferrill's Auto Parts, Inc.:** 18306-Hwy. 99, Lynnwood, Wash. 98037. Phone 1-800-421-3147, 206-778-3147; Fax 206-771-3147. Hours Mon.-Fri. 8 a.m.-5:30 p.m., Sat. 8 a.m.-5 p.m. Customers may browse yard. Mail-order service. Specializes in

domestic and import models from 1976-92. Approximately 1,600 vehicles in yard. Three locations. Computerized inventory. In business over 40 years.

**Fitz Auto Parts:** 24000 Hwy. 9, Woodinville, Wash. 98072. Phone 206-483-1212. Hours Mon.-Sat. 8:30 a.m.-5 p.m. Mail-order service. Specializes in products from Ford, GM, Chrysler/Jeep, plus European and Japanese vehicles. Approximately 2,500 vehicles in yard. In business over 60 years.

**I-5 Auto & Truck Parts:** (also known as Classic Cars, Ltd.) 190 Estep Rd., Chehalis, Wash. 98532. Phone 206-262-3550, 1-800-551-4489. Sam or Dave Clark, or Frank Carson. Mail order services. Hours Mon.-Sat. 9 a.m.-5:30 p.m.

**Jackson's Hudsons:** Hunzeker Rd., Yakima, Wash. Phone 509-966-2341. Call before visiting. Selling whole cars. Approximately 40 vehicles mostly from the 1950s. Few Nashes and Cadillacs.

**Part Time Auto Wrecking:** HC 01, Box 620, Ilwaco, Wash. 98624. Phone 206-642-4852. Hours Mon.-Fri. 9 a.m.-5 p.m., Sat. 9 a.m.-noon. Customers may browse yard. Yard specializes in 1970-80 models. Anyone wishing older parts for '50s iron should submit a specific parts list. Approximately 300 vehicles in yard with a flow of about 250 per year. In business since 1980.

**Ray's Auto Wrecking:** 2707 100th St., Everett, Wash. 98208. Phone 360-337-4056, 360-337-4656. Hours 9 a.m.-5 p.m. From I-5, take 128th St. exit, go east to 100th St. and turn right. About 1/2 mile on the left. No parts shipping.

**Rowland's Antique Auto Parts:** Jerry Rowland, P.O. Box 387, Zillah, Wash. 98953. Phone 509-829-5026. Mail order only. No browsing permitted. Specializing in Lincoln and Mercury parts from 1939-69. Most are 1950s and '60s. Can be shipped all over the world. In business over 25 years.

**Vintage Auto Parts, Inc.:** 24300 Hwy 9, Woodinville, Wash. 98072. Phone 206-486-0777; Fax 206-486-0778. Hours Mon.-Fri. 8 a.m.-5 p.m., Sat. 9 a.m.-4 p.m. The largest stock of NOS parts 1920-70 in the U.S. We ship anywhere. Since 1960.

## WEST VIRGINIA

**Antique Auto Parts:** C.A. Smith, Jr. P.O. Box 64, Elkview, W.Va. 25071. Phone 304-965-1821. Hours Mon.-Sat. 9 a.m.-dusk. Inventory list available. Customers may browse yard. Mail-order service. Specializes in 1935-69, most makes. Approximately 134 vehicles in yard.

## WISCONSIN

**All Auto Acres:** W3862 Hwy. 16, Rio, Wis. 53960. Phone 414-992-5362, 1-800-637-4661 (WI). Roger or Renee Gavitt. Hours Mon.-Fri. 8 a.m.-5 p.m., Sat. 8 a.m.-noon. Customers may browse yard. Mail orders

accepted. Specializes in 1955-85 American cars and light trucks. New replacement fenders, doors, etc., in fiberglass and metal. Approximately 2,000 vehicles in yard. In business over nine years.

**Bradley Auto Inc.:** Ke Wegener, 2026 Hwy. A., West Bend, Wis. 53095. Phone 414-334-4653, 414-334-4066. Hours Mon.-Fri. 8 a.m.-5 p.m., Sat. 8 a.m.-noon. Mail-order service. Specializes in American, imports, light-duty trucks, 1975-current. Approximately 1,000 vehicles in yard. Special interest and collectibles bought, sold, and traded.

**C.L. Chase Used Auto and Truck Parts:** Carl Chase, W 10416 County C, Camp Douglas, Wis. 54618. Phone 608-427-6734. Hours 8 a.m.-6 p.m., seven days a week. Over 5,000 cars and trucks from 1920 to present, including muscle cars and parts.

**Golden Sands Salvage:** 501 Airport Rd., Boscobel, Wis. 53805. Phone 608-375-5353. Keith Swenson, owner. Hours Mon.-Fri. 8:30 a.m.-5:30 p.m., Sat. 8:30 a.m.-noon. Inventory list available. Customers may browse yard. Mail order services. Specializing in all makes, '30s to '70s. Approximately 300 collectible cars. Approximately 1,000 cars in the yard. In business over five years.

**Helgesen Antique Auto Parts:** Rt. 6, Janesville, Wis. 53545. Fax 608-756-0469.

**Jacks Auto Ranch:** Jack Bender, 6848 N. Islandview Rd., Watertown, Wis. 53094. Phone 920-699-2521; Fax 920-699-2985. Hours Mon.- Fri. 8 a.m.-5 p.m., Sat. 8 a.m.-noon. Over 3,000 cars 1930-70s. Ship post office, UPS, truck and international. Large or small parts.

**Ray's Automotive Ent., Inc.:** 605 W. Bayfield St., Washburn, Wis. 54891. Phone 715-373-2669. Ray. Hours Mon.-Sat. 8 a.m.-5 p.m. Customers may browse yard. Specializes in all foreign and domestic cars, trucks 1960s and up. Approximately 1,500 vehicles in yard. Towing, body repairs, frame work offered. In business over 22 years.

**Ray's Auto Repair/Salvage:** Ron Parent, Rt. 1, Box 85, Sanborn Ave., Ashland, Wis. 54806. Phone 715-682-6505. Hours Mon.-Fri. 9 a.m.-5 p.m., Sat. 9 a.m.-2 p.m. Customers may browse yard. Specializes in 1964 and up. Approximately 250 vehicles in yard. Services offered are exhaust shop, rebuilding brake shoes. In business over 30 years.

**Dale Remington Salvage Yard:** Corner of C & TT, Eau Claire, Wis. 54701. Phone 715-834-2560.

**Seward Auto Salvage, Inc.:** Hank Seward, 2506 E. Vincent Rd., Milton, Wis. 53563. Phone 608-752-5166. Hours Mon.-Sat. 8 a.m.-5 p.m. Approximately 2,500 cars and trucks, 1937 to present on 37 acres. Many odd and orphan cars, plus some old foreign. Sorted out and kept clean. Browsers welcome. Send SASE.

**Somerset Auto Salvage & Repair:** 1920 Hwy. 35 N, Somerset, Wis. 54025. Phone 715-247-5136. Hours Mon.-Sat. 8 a.m.-5 p.m. Specializes in all cars from old to new, foreign and domestic and pickups. Approximately 1,000 vehicles in yard. Complete service on engines and drive trains. In business over 15 years.

**Van's Auto Salvage:** Rt. 2, Box 164, Waupun, Wis. 53963. Phone 414-324-2481. Ted or Larry Vander Woude. Hours Tues.-Fri. 9 a.m.-5 p.m., Sat. 8 a.m.-noon. Customers may browse yard. Mail-order service. Specializes in makes and models from 1947-76, plus a few in the '30s. Approximately 4,000 vehicles in yard. In business over 27 years.

**Wiese Auto Recycling, Inc.:** Rt. 1, Box 32, Hwy. T.W., Theresa, Wis. 53091. Phone 414-488-3030. Bob, Chuck or Gail Wiese. Hours Mon.-Fri. 8 a.m.-5 p.m., Sat. 8 a.m.-noon. Partial inventory list available. Customers may browse yard. Mail-order service. Specializes in mostly American models from the late '60s to present; some foreign. Approximately 500 vehicles in yard. Offers repair, body and frame work, plus towing service and storage. In business over 21 years.

**Zeb's Salvage:** Mike Kasperek, N3181 Bernitt Rd., Tigerton, Wis. 54486. Phone 715-754-5885. Hours Mon.-Sat. 8 a.m.-5 p.m. Customer may browse yard. Mail order services for small items only. Specializes in most makes and models '30s to '70s. Approximately 900 vehicles in yard. Offers engine work, valve jobs, snow plowing and welding. In business over nine years.

# CANADA

**Aldon Auto Salvage Ltd.:** Ian and Terry Carter, Hwy 831, Lamont, Alb., Canada T0B 2R0. Phone 403-895-2524; Fax 403-895-7555. Hours Mon.-Fri. 8 a.m.-5:30 p.m., Sat. 8:30 a.m.-3 p.m. Yard specializes in all North American cars and light trucks, 1940-95. Approximately 4,000 vehicles in yard. Offers towing, engine rebuilding, parts locating & delivery service. In business over 26 years.

**C.R. Auto:** Randy Berfelo, Box 237, Hay Lakes, Alb., Canada T0B 1W0. Located 38 miles southeast of Edmonton, Alb., Canada. Phone 403-878-3263. Hours Mon.-Fri. 8 a.m.-7 p.m., Sat. 9 a.m.-6 p.m. Mail-order service. Specializes in Cadillacs only, 1947-79. Bumpers for most Cadillacs. Firm offers restoration work for Cadillacs only. Approximately 240 vehicles in yard. In business over five years.

**Elliott Auto Parts:** 4752 Highway 2, near Newtonville, Ont., Canada. Phone 905-786-2255. Take Highway 401 to exit 448, travel north to Highway 2, turn east, go one mile. Hours weekdays 8 a.m.-6 p.m., Sat. 9 a.m.-1 p.m.

**Fawcett Motor Carriage Co.:** 106 Palmerston Ave., Whitby, Ont., Canada L1N 3E5. Phone 905-668-4446; (Toronto) 905-686-1412; Fax 905-668-3203. Hours Mon.-Sat. 7 a.m.-5 p.m. Visitors are welcome to tour the yard, with permission. In business over 40 years.

**Freddie Beach Restorations:** 1834 Woodstock Road, Fredericton, NB, Canada E3C 1L4. Phone 506-450-9074; Fax 506-459-0708. Hours Mon.- Fri. 6 p.m.-9 p.m., Sat. 10 a.m.-5 p.m. Supplying restoration and high performance parts and accessories for all makes and models since 1994. vallise@city.fredericton.hb.ca.

**Raymond M. Ganser:** P.O. Box 357, Provost, Alb., Canada T0B 3S0. Phone 403-753-6797. Hours 8 a.m.-8 p.m. Parting out 1926-29 Chevys, 1927 Chrysler 50, 1928 Pontiacs, 1928 Whippets, 1928 Essex, 1928 Plymouth.

**Roy Graham's Studebaker Parts:** RR No. 4, Marmora, Ont., Canada K0K 2M0. Phone 613-395-0353. Visitors need to call in advance.

**Minaker's Auto Parts:** Paul Minaker, 3073 Cty. Rd. 10, Box 100, Milford, Ont., Canada K0K 2P0. Phone 613-476-4547; Fax 613-476-1565. Hours Mon., Tues., Wed., Fri. 9 a.m.-5 p.m., Thurs. 9 a.m.-noon, Sat. 9 a.m.-4 p.m. A 50 acre yard with over 3,000 vehicles from 1925 to present. Lots of NOS parts. Founded in 1925.

**Reg's Storage:** Reg Hillgardner, 10820 Winterburn Rd. N.W., Edmonton, Alb., Canada T5S 2C3. Phone 403-447-3610. Hours Mon.-Fri. 8 a.m.-6 p.m., Sat. 8 a.m.-4 p.m. Inventory list available. Specializes in North American cars and light trucks from 1940 to 1986. Approximately 500 vehicles in yard. In business 33 years.

**Reynolds Museum:** Bruce Olson, 4110-57 St., Wetaskiwin, Alb., Canada T9A 2B6. Phone 403-352-6201; Fax 403-352-4666. Hours 8 a.m.-4 p.m., Mon.-Fri. year round. Over 400 unrestored, weathered and parts cars and trucks 1918 to 1958 for sale. Also, tractors, steam engines, stationary engines, etc. Some lists available. stanreynoldssales@incentre.net.